TRANS-EUROPEAN TELECOMMUNICATION NETWORKS

The provision of advanced telecommunication networks is increasingly pivotal in determining an economy's performance. Colin Turner's ground-breaking study examines the importance of these networks within the EU and questions their role in promoting economic regeneration and renewal in Europe.

Examining the nature of telecommunication networks and the rationale for the development of trans-European networks, the study explores the features networks need to exhibit if they are to complement the broad themes of Europe's industrial policy, and demonstrates the economic importance of advanced telecommunications to business. The final chapters of the volume offer an analysis of the technology associated with the three chosen priorities of the EU in the development of advanced telecommunication infrastructure:

- the Integrated Services Digital Network (ISDN)
- the development of telematic networks
- the development of broadband networks

Colin Turner is an ex-merchant banker who is currently a lecturer in Economics and International Studies at the University of Lincolnshire and Humberside. He has published widely in the field of European Economics, and is the co-author, with D. Johnson, of a text upon Trans-European Networks. He has published articles in many journals, including *Telecommunications Policy*.

ROUTLEDGE STUDIES IN THE EUROPEAN ECONOMY

TRANS-EUROPEAN TELECOMMUNICATION NETWORKS

The challenges for industrial policy

Colin Turner

London and New York

First published 1997
by Routledge
11 New Fetter Lane, London EC4P 4EE

Simultaneously published in the USA and Canada
by Routledge
29 West 35th Street, New York, NY 10001

Typeset in Garamond by Keystroke, Jacaranda Lodge, Wolverhampton
Printed and bound in Great Britain by TJ Press International Ltd, Padstow, Cornwall

British Library Cataloguing in Publication Data
A catalogue record for this book is available from the British Library

Library of Congress Cataloging in Publication Data
Turner, Colin, 1967–
Trans-European telecommunication networks : the challenges for
industrial policy / Colin Turner.
p.   cm.
Includes bibliographical references.
1. Telecommunication–Europe. 2. Telecommunication–Economic
aspects–Europe. I. Title.
HE8084.T87   1997
384'.094–dc21   97–3705
CIP

ISBN 0–415–16186–X

CONTENTS

CONTENTS

LIST OF FIGURES AND TABLES

FIGURES

TABLES

PREFACE

There is perhaps currently no greater policy challenge within the EU than that to promote sustainable employment and growth. A necessary precursor to achieving this objective is for policy-makers to stimulate the conditions under which enterprises operating within the European economy can attain a state of global competitiveness. Creating such conditions has been the primary focus in developing industrial strategies at the national and supranational levels. It is within this context that the importance of generating advanced telecommunication infrastructures in an integrated manner across the EU emerges. Pushing the development of these networks as a promoter of such changes is ultimately the theme of this text.

Many of the industrial challenges faced by European states are sourced from the nature and form of structural and logistical change within their economies. This change is derived from the increased prominence of information and communication within economies. One of the major foci of industrial strategy is to harness such changes to promote the future and sustained economic success of European economies. This action has found its most prominent expression in actions to develop the 'information society' where a mature information culture is sought across Europe's varied social and economic structures. Such changes need to be underpinned by the development of a complementary telecommunications infrastructure. The commonality of these challenges has helped focus policy-makers upon the development of these networks on a transnational level.

The rationale of this text is to help contribute to the understanding of these processes. The central theme is upon policies to establish the advanced telecommunications infrastructure as a precursor of the shift to the information society. Inevitably in addressing this core issue the reader needs to be aware of the broader issues involved such as the information society, the increased prominence of information and communications technologies and the accompanying global challenges. Throughout the text a number of technical terms related to telecommunications are used. I have explained those technologies which are integral to strategies for the development of the network. Other terms that are less pivotal are left unexplained and may need to be cross-referenced with basic texts on telecommunications.

The initial chapters seek to perform two roles. The first is to understand the role of advanced telecommunication networks within Europe's industrial strategy. This requires an examination of the nature of telecommunication networks, of structural changes provoked by information, the rationale for the development of trans-European networks, and the features they need to exhibit if they are to complement the broad themes of Europe's industrial strategy. Second, the economic importance of advanced telecommunications to enterprises is explored. These two themes are inevitably interlinked as policy-makers would clearly not prioritise these infrastructures if they were not believed to be of benefit. Many of these benefits are linked to the evolving internationalisation of economies and enterprises.

The strategy to realise these networks is very much a derivative of the EU's market-led industrial strategy. The incremental liberalisation is envisaged as being the major deliverer of the finance necessary for network development. Despite this, policy-makers seek to complement the process to ensure that networks develop as a broader economic resource. A further feature of this strategy has been the number of competitive and pre-competitive alliances that are prevalent in EU network development. Thus overall the development of networks will be a mix of public and private sector action and of commercial and non-commercial endeavour. The combination of these actions and the perceived importance of the development of networks requires the EU to perform a network management role in the evolution of advanced telecommunications infrastructures.

Thereafter the particular technologies related to the development of trans-European telecommunication networks are explored. The choice of these chapters reflects the three chosen priorities of the EU in the development of advanced telecommunications infrastructure. The first is the Integrated Services Digital Network (ISDN) which reflects the desire of policy-makers to achieve greater value added for enterprises and other economic agents from existing infrastructure. The second is the development of telematic networks which represent the EU's desire to ensure that advanced infrastructures deliver a content which promotes the broad industrial priorities of the European states. Finally, the development of broadband networks in the EU is explored. Within the current time frame and set of economic priorities, this represents the final stage of network evolution. In the light of these developments, the final chapter explores some concluding themes.

GLOSSARY

ACTS   Advanced Communications Telecommunications and Services.

ATM   Asynchronous Transfer Mode.

BT   British Telecom.

CEC   Commission of the European Communities.

CEPT   European Conference on Postal and Telecommunication Administration.

DGXIII   Directorate General Thirteen.

DT   Deutsche Telekom.

EIB   European Investment Bank.

EII   European Information Infrastructure.

E-ISDN   European ISDN.

Esprit   European Strategic Programme for research into information technology.

ENS   European Nervous System.

ETSI   European Telecommunications Standards Institute.

EU   European Union.

FT   France Telecom.

G7   Group of Seven states.

GII   Global Information Infrastructure.

IBC   Integrated Broadband Communications.

ICTs   Information and Communication Technologies.

ISDN   Integrated Digital Services Network.

IT	Information Technology.
JAMES	Joint ATM Experiment on European Services.
Mbp/s	Megabits per second.
MNCs/MNEs	Multi-national companies/enterprises.
N-ISDN	Narrowband ISDN.
ONP	Open Network Provision.
PPPs	Public–Private Partnerships.
PSTN	Public Switched Telecommunications Network.
PTOs	Public Telecommunications Operators.
R&D	Research and Development.
RACE	Research into Advanced Communications in Europe.
RTD	Research and Technological Development.
SDH	Synchronous Digital Hierarchy.
SEM	Single European Market.
SMEs	Small and Medium-sized Enterprises.
STAR	Special Telecommunications Action for Regional Development.
TENs	Trans-European Networks.
VAN	Value Added Networks.
VPNs	Virtual Private Networks.

1

TRANS-EUROPEAN TELECOMMUNICATION NETWORKS AND THE RISE OF THE INFORMATION ECONOMY

INTRODUCTION

Within modern economies, information is playing an increasingly prominent role. How an economy and the enterprises within it use and manipulate information is becoming crucial in determining competitiveness on a global stage. A major focus for industrial policy is the promotion of efficient and effective delivery and utilisation of information.

The aims of this chapter are to examine the key aspects of trans-European telecommunication networks (telecom-TENs) and the environment within which they are emerging in order:

- to understand the nature of industrial policy and infrastructure networks and to comprehend, initially, the interlinkages between the two;
- to understand the economic changes promoted by the rise of the information revolution;
- to understand the characteristics that telecommunication networks must exhibit if they are to complement these changes and the broad industrial policy objectives that are a response to such phenomena.

Thereafter the nature of telecom-TENs is explored as a precursor to understanding how the broad industrial policy objectives of the EU are reflected within the TENs criteria. These criteria are the characteristics that these networks must exhibit if, according to the Treaty upon European Union, they are be truly trans-European. The extent to which these criteria are met by the EU's priority telecommunications networks will determine, in no small part, the extent to which these telecom-TENs are complementary to Europe's strategy for economic development and regeneration.

INDUSTRIAL POLICY AND THE IMPORTANCE OF TRANS-EUROPEAN NETWORKS

A basic function of industrial policy is to push, manage and control the forces of change within the modern economy. The changes promoted by the rise of information and communication technologies (ICTs) in industrialised states are symptomatic of the emerging information economy (Greenop 1995). Such transformations rely upon the increased importance of information in socio-economic processes. This places great emphasis upon utilising ICTs right throughout the economic strata.

Many decision-makers, at both national and supranational level, believe continued economic success will be linked to the ability to utilise information and communication in an effective and efficient manner.[1] The nature of the information economy is the osmotic tendency of all economic activities to be associated with production, consumption and distribution of information. This refers not only to new industries but also to those whose competitive position is threatened by newly emerging industrialising states. In modern economies, industrial policy is tending to focus upon accelerating these changes to ensure the sustenance and maintenance of their relative position.

Such changes are also symptomatic of increases in global trade and competition; a trend to which industrial policy is ultimately seeking to respond. The reaction to such changes has been to seek to work with market adjustment rather than delay its onset. This stems from the perceived failure of activism which has bred a realisation that competitiveness cannot be created but only achieved from within the framework of markets (Hall 1986).

Competitiveness and its maintenance lie at the heart of industrial policy. Competitiveness is basically 'the capacity of business, industries, regions, nations or supranational associations, exposed and remaining exposed to international competition to secure a relatively high return to factors of production and relatively high employment levels on a sustainable basis'.[2] A competitive position is not a 'state' but a 'process'. Economies need to respond flexibly to what global economic forces are telling them if they are to maintain their competitive position. The increased application of ICTs to all parts of the economy is symptomatic of such changes and is believed to deliver competitive 'flexible' enterprises into the new millennium. Within this changing global economy and policy environment the information economy is emerging.

Policy is stressing competition as a precursor of change. As Bangemann says, 'nothing is better for competitiveness than competition itself'.[3] Such a stance is reflected at the heart of the SEM (Single European Market) initiative which is based upon the desire to enhance the mobility of goods, services, capital and labour; the so-called four freedoms. By promoting the more efficient use and reallocation of resources, the development of the SEM was a supply side initiative for the European economy. Consequently, in accordance with the conclusions of Porter (1990), the promotion of more intense competition is seen as pivotal in promoting industrial competitiveness (see Table 1.1).

2

Within this general policy framework, the EU foresees its role as a 'catalyst and path breaker for innovation'. In practice this means that it performs a largely passive and co-ordinative role. Any 'supranational' activism is, by and large, merely sanctioning as compatible with EC law those measures undertaken by the member state. Any activism by the states has to be justified in terms of the successful realisation of the EU's objectives. This underlines the perspective that the best promoters of change and competitiveness are firms themselves.

Reich (1991) noted, 'What is the role of a nation in the emerging global economy in which borders are ceasing to exist? Rather than increasing the profitability of corporations flying the flag, or enlarging the worldwide holdings of its citizens, a nation's economic role is to improve its citizens' standard of living by enhancing the value of what they contribute to the world economy.'[4] The role of the state in such a scenario is inevitably prone to change. Policy must be focused on developing a strategic response to such changes, working with them rather than against them to ensure the success of the economy. Such policies mean that the operational problems are left to enterprises and strategic guidance is offered to oversee the interplay of market forces. Within such a policy stance 'planning and the market are complements rather than substitutes'.[5] In this broad context, the state is a passive promoter of change, seeking to encourage enterprises to behave in manner that is in the generic interests of the economy as a whole.

Attaining and maintaining competitiveness is not in the whim of the state. Competitiveness is a relative and dynamic concept and therefore the preoccupation of states should be in creating the conditions under which competitiveness can be sustained. Any strategy for 'industry' should seek to avoid short-term political measures and focus upon those that meet the longer-term needs of the economy. This implies that a full account of the role of enterprise and how the state will complement such market-driven actions needs to be assessed. Hence co-operation between enterprises and authorities is needed to ensure that the policy develops in a manner which is conducive to practical needs. Such a strategy emphasises the supply-side preconditions for international competitiveness. The two substantial documents upon industrial policy that have emerged in the wake of the SEM have stressed such themes.[6] The key issues in both documents were in setting a supply-side agenda for the EU and ensuring that market forces work to the common advantage. Consequently much of the action is based around ensuring that markets provide the adjustment needed in the desired fashion. The three key themes stressed are indicated in Table 1.1.

The prerequisites for change provide the foundation for the persistent competitiveness of the economy. The catalysts are the actual predicted causes of change. The accelerators of adjustment are those that will enhance the effects of the catalysts.

These themes reflect a broad set of horizontal policies to meet the common interests of states and exhibit the belief that 'sectoral policies . . . do not form an effective instrument to promote structural adjustment'.[7] Accordingly change is promoted by increasing the intensity of competition from both internal and

Table 1.1 Industrial policy themes for the EU

Prerequisites for structural adjustment	Catalysts	Accelerators of adjustment
• Securing a competitive environment • Maintaining a stable economic environment • High educational attainments especially scientific and technical expertise • Knowledge and its effective and efficient use in human resources • Better organisation of production • Economic and social cohesion • Environment protection	• Single European Market • Freer world trade	• Increasing technological capacity • Small and medium-sized enterprises • Developing business services • Utilising human resources more efficiently • Promoting intangible investment • Industrial co-operation • Modern role for public authorities • Fair competition

Source: Commission of the European Communities, 1990a

external sources. According to the European Commission, these catalysts need to be complemented by investment in human capital, cohesion and the more efficient organisation of production. These themes were developed in the *White Paper Upon Growth, Competitiveness and Employment,*[8] which addressed the problems of the European economy in a thematic way, stressing the interlinkages between the three subjects. It underlined the increasingly prevalent view that only more open markets could provide the solution required. The basis of the strategy is to seek to implement the issues addressed within the document as a basis for a competitive EU. Consequently there is emphasis upon macro-economic stability, structural change (the information society), enhancing the SEM and developing small and medium-sized enterprises (SMEs).

The rise of Trans-European networks

The criteria set out in Table 1.1 indicate the general framework within which TENs are expected to emerge. Indeed there are elements of this policy throughout the TENs programme (see Chapter 2). TENs are there to enhance the catalytic effects, to create the right conditions for smooth and speedy structural adjustment and to respond to the requests of the market. Thus the development of TENs complements many aspects of the EU's market-led industrial policy, something that is reflected within the TENs criteria.

TENs, as a policy issue, initially emerged as a complementary factor which enhanced the four freedoms facilitated by the SEM. The role of TENs was to support broader economic changes within the European economy by amplifying

4

the effects of the legislative changes facilitated by the SEM. Consequently their economic impact is based upon attaining two key objectives:

- mobility: assisting trade and factor flows across borders;
- accessibility: ensuring that all relevant economic operators have access to these networks.

The priority of the SEM as a sole initial justification for the development of TENs has been diluted over time. Now these networks are expected to play a much broader role in the economic development and regeneration of the European economy.

The role of infrastructure in economic and technological development is well documented.[9] Within the context of the trend towards the Europeanisation and, eventually, globalisation of economies there is a realisation that the economic welfare of states lies beyond their own specified geographical/political space. Infrastructure design and development have to stress the needs of economic development over a broader geographical plane – in this case Europe. The important implication is that physical interconnection and interoperability of national networks needs to be assured.

If the legislative changes are to work to the broader competitive advantage of the EU, then it is important to see how the reorganisation of production promoted by the SEM could work its way fully through the EU economy (CEC 1990b). Legislation may allow mobility and access in theory but unless the networks can support such movements the impact of the SEM will be, at least partially, dissipated. Consequently the development of TENs and the competitiveness effects of the SEM are interconnected. In combination they could lead to a fulsome development of the network economy and enable firms to reorganise more efficiently across national borders. The rise of the network economy requires a set of supporting infrastructures acting as delivery channels for services to meet the increasing complexity and depth of interactions and the forces of integration that result.

At the heart, TENs initiative is a scheme for market integration and economic and social cohesion by reducing in temporal terms the distance between locations. Importantly, 'the aim of this policy is not to re-design the European (infrastructure) system . . . into a uniform whole but . . . to achieve interconnecting national subsystems'.[10] This does not imply a drastic overhaul of the system but a re-establishment of the priorities to stress new economic themes and issues.

In terms of both infrastructure and inter-firm relationships, networks are proving to be the focus of interaction upon which further justification for integration can be based.[11] National borders are becoming irrelevant for the operation of business. The efficiency of business therefore needs to be supported by a set of networks to aid relationship formation and to aid other forms of transnational interaction. This creates a tendency towards an osmotic process of integration. In short, integration is described not for political ends but as a practical response to the needs of the modern economy.

As a key business input, the Commission argues that the persistently high price of network services (relative to the EU's major competitors) has limited Europe's competitiveness.[12] Such costs have been exaggerated in part by inadequate infrastructure as well as a lack of competition in the services provided. The Competitiveness Advisory Group highlighted how the quality of infrastructure is proving to be the single most important factor influencing multinational investment. Competition within this sector represents a 'win–win' situation for the EU in terms of better quality infrastructure and improved derived value in terms of services provided. Europe's strategy for telecom-TENs further reflects the perceived economic importance of information and communication within enterprises.

THE ECONOMIC IMPORTANCE OF INFORMATION AND COMMUNICATION[13]

Growth is the result of the creation and accumulation of physical factors of production and knowledge. Knowledge is playing a leading role in determining a region's economic success as the generation of new ideas stimulates economic development. Within this context the development of ICTs implies a desire to fulfil a precise economic need. Indeed the entire development of modes of communication implies a need to transmit information between parties that lie upon the same network and that the information imparted must possess some economic or social value. Communication is wanted because it delivers information and information is wanted because it delivers knowledge. Ultimately we are dealing with a series of derived demands that respond to the needs of economic agents. In any market the acquisition of knowledge is essential in making decisions about strategy, frequently in the light of those being developed elsewhere. The possession of knowledge therefore requires a means of distribution. This is especially important in global environments where the economic significance of information is more spatially valued than ever before. Modern ICTs and the network economy have emerged in response to the value associated with information and communication. ICTs are a means of ensuring that information can be as perfect as commercially and technologically feasible (given communication technology). Within the modern enterprise, information should be utilised to maximise commercial advantage. Thus ICTs seek to ensure that those who possess information have the potential to employ it effectively.

Within the market economy, the role of information is vital in sending signals to agents to act in a way that is to the individual's good. Information is what all actors will respond to once they are aware of it. Over time an entire branch of economics has built up on information dealing with issues such as moral hazard and expectations. All parts of this branch of economics stress the importance of information and its effect when its distribution and availability is either asymmetric or just unknown.

In an era of profound structural and economic change, information and its effects are now at a premium. The uncertainty created by structural change requires the development of organisations that can utilise information to minimise the uncertainty derived from such altering scenarios. This extends not just to knowledge delivered by technology but knowledge of technology itself. Within firms it is clear that there is a process of discovery, whether in response to internal developments (via research and development, for example) or to external events. This further increases the premium placed upon information and its dissemination throughout the enterprise\economy.

The creation of information will tend to occur to a point where it delivers value added that exceeds or is equal to the cost of its generation. Generally the challenge is to ensure that the private production of information is sufficient to ensure that markets function effectively. What is important within this context is the quality of the knowledge produced and its lifespan. The competitiveness of an area is linked to its knowledge and the extent to which its knowledge gives it a coherent advantage over other areas. This explains the importance of science and research and development (R&D) in competitiveness. These are the factors that improve knowledge and once disseminated create enhanced competitiveness. Such an analysis directly parallels Schumpetarian examination of the process of discovery. As such the success of an economy can be determined by the quality of knowledge aided by research and development. Changing knowledge and information create the so-called creative process of destruction. This underlines the importance of information and knowledge to modern economies as factors promoting economic and structural change (Drucker 1993).

THE INFORMATION REVOLUTION AND INDUSTRIAL POLICY

According to Nijkamp *et al.* (1994)[14] changes in the uses of ICTs by enterprises have been the main engine of growth within the global economy since the 1970s and are a direct derivative of the industrial revolution. Industrial policy has focused increasingly upon the application of this logistical revolution to maintain the global positioning of indigenous enterprises. The more information becomes seen as an economic resource in its own right, the greater the stakes involved in ensuring its effective and efficient utilisation by all relevant actors. Thus policy seeks to push this aspect of structural change as a necessary precursor of sustained competitiveness (Bell 1976).

Negroponte (1994)[15] describes the industrial age as being about the movement of atoms, for example manufactured goods, newspapers and books. The information age will be about the movement of information in the form of digital bits. A key feature of a revolution, any revolution, is that it tends to destabilise the society into which it is working. To aid this an information society has to grow, becoming one in which these changes do not isolate portions of the population and therefore wealth creation is balanced with social well-being (Greenop 1995). The information society has to be based, initially at least, upon utilising information and communication as an economic resource and a social good.[16]

The rise of the 'knowledge based economy' (Machlup 1962) is characterised by what is termed the increased division of economic activity into production tasks (i.e. the production and distribution process) and information tasks (i.e. tasks associated with the co-ordination and manipulation of production tasks) (Jonscher 1983). The central contention is that the latter is becoming more important than the former. Activities that are knowledge and information based are becoming core strategic resources essential for prolonged economic development within post-industrial economies.[17] Such changes are inextricably linked with the broader diffusion of ICTs.[18]

Inevitably the building block for these changes is the telecommunications network (Bell 1976). The improved value added from the advances in technology will only be as great as the capability of the network to support such changes. In many cases network technology has been, and will continue to be, the facilitator of such changes. The ICT infrastructure has to be in place to ensure that all parts of the economic area feel the benefit from its wider adoption. The spread of ICTs and the telecommunications network work in conjunction with time–space and cost–space convergence. The telecommunications network, by passively promoting such convergence, underpins its role in assisting harmonious economic development (Jannelle 1991). To support such changes four basic criteria have to be in place (Hudson 1994):

- accessibility: the network is available to the widest range of socio-economic groups;
- equity: non-discriminatory use of the network in terms of availability and price;
- connectivity: a precursor of universal communications;
- flexibility: networks must be able to accept, adopt and adapt to new technologies.

The structural changes in the telecommunications sector are being driven by technological, market and institutional dynamics,[19] as well as the rise of new economic relationships.[20] The new entry and competition fostered by governments are altering the face of telecommunications. This is a sector that is no longer a true public service but a true economic resource that needs to differentiate between the requirements of different users. The provision of telecommunications networks has the capability to offer many advantages to many regions. But their ability to enjoy such benefits depends upon the competence of economies to invest in the right infrastructure. The drivers behind the broader provision of the network have to be understood. The effects on the economy will only be as good as the ability of the new ICTs to diffuse themselves within the economic structures of the area concerned. Capello (1994) indicates three factors that will contribute to this:

- dynamic externalities – where the desire for services is dependent upon how many others use the network, thus determining its usefulness;
- learning processes – how quickly users become accustomed to the use of new technologies will determine, in part, the demand for ICTs;
- technological requirements – the physical capabilities of the network to support such changes and deliver the functionality required.

Complementary to these factors (Antonelli 1992) are:

- the macro-economic situation: the ability of the firms to afford the necessary investment in ICTs;
- the epidemic of technology: the spread of new and evolving technology throughout the economic structures of a state;
- supply dynamics: how innovative and responsive are firms to user requirements;
- user-value associated with the network: the extent to which the service capabilities afforded by the network are exploited by the end user.

The rise of the information age carries many industrial policy implications from labour skills and regional development through to the emergence of new enterprises that service these structural changes.[21] Such trends underline the importance of infrastructure in economic development.[22] The information age requires alternative forms of infrastructure to support these new modes of interaction. The delivery channels (a network of information and telecommunication networks) for information and communication are going to be pivotal in the competitive positioning of enterprises.

COMMON INFORMATION AREA AND THE INFORMATION SOCIETY

The Common Information Area (CIA) is a response to the industrial challenges[23] posed by freer global and regional trade. Its aim is to ensure that the free mobility of information complements mobility and accessibility on a broader scale. Information is a facilitator and a business resource; without free movement the full benefits of the freer trade will not be felt. The basis of the CIA is a series of telecommunications networks that are used to support a wide range of information services. Inevitably a CIA has to be founded upon a set of agreed standards and protocols to support the flow of information across borders in response to external economic stimuli. Part of the need to establish this network is the interpenetration of ICTs and the rest of Europe's industrial sector.

The CIA should be seen as a common resource that deliberately excludes no one from its reach. In many ways it will provide the link between the attainment of economic integration and the promotion of technological development associated with the information society. Consequently it is important to underline that successful moves towards the SEM, and to EMU thereafter, rely upon promoting the technological development of all parts of the European space. The CIA should evolve as the demands placed upon it change. Initially this can involve existing networks such as the Internet which can be complemented by the transition to ISDN and eventually IBC.

The CIA's complementarity to the information society has to be regarded in many ways as the reason for its development. The information society involves the mass consumption of advanced, and ultimately broadband, services. Thus the CIA is the means for their delivery throughout the economic space. The development of the information society is a key policy aim of European states. It is the means via which these states complete the transformation to post-industrial society. Such a transformation implies the development of a new means of attaining international competitiveness. Success will be based upon renewing and assessing labour skills and developing the right industrial sectors to attain and maintain a competitive advantage within the information and communication sectors and beyond.

Despite all the hype surrounding the information superhighway, it has to be remembered that at the heart its development is about attaining and maintaining economic success in to the twenty-first century. Policy focus has been upon creating a mass market for the potential of the network. The success of this strategy is only as good as the degree of commitment offered to it by the relevant actors. The expectations of the economic impact of the information society are high. It is a strong vision that requires concerted action in its attainment. The information society is not an end in itself, but is a catalyst to encourage innovation to improve commercial performance. Overall the development of the information society will emerge as a result of interactions between political authorities, users, information providers, service providers, network operators and the manufacturers of hardware and software. Such a trend underlines the belief that the development of the information society is dependent upon the emergence of new players and upon existing actors establishing new roles and functions for themselves (Greenop 1995). It is within this framework that the private and public sectors will interact to promote the onset of the information society.

NATURE AND FORM OF TELECOMMUNICATION NETWORKS

The ability of telecommunication networks to support these changes is based upon updating the basic building blocks of a network to enable it to support a broader range of more advanced applications and services. These features in combination will determine its capabilities in terms of what it can achieve and to what extent it can support all the activities required.

There are three basic features of any network: nodes, links and services. In terms of telecom-TENs, the development of telecommunication networks is focused upon three basic factors:

- nodes, ensuring that technology within them develops in an interoperable fashion;
- links between nodes are updated to increase bandwidth and capacity needed to support the anticipated economic requirements;
- services and applications develop in a manner that aids the industrial policy objectives.

This third aspect is the most important feature economically and represents the ultimate source of value from the network for users.

Additionally it is useful to delineate in spatial terms the telecommunications network between local and wide area networks. Local area networks (LANs) are exclusively private networks designed to serve a number of users within a limited geographical area such as a building. Their limited size means that they are often the focus for the initial development of technology. Wide Area Networks (WANs), with which TENs in telecommunications are largely concerned, include both private and public networks operating over an expansive geographical area.

A number of other features of telecommunications need to be noted (Antonelli 1992). First, networks are comprised of an array of heterogeneous technical components supplied by a range of suppliers. All these components are interrelated and need to support each other in order to develop a homogeneous network. Second, any network is part of a global network. Third, telecommunication infrastructures are based on a derived demand. They are wanted for what they deliver to enterprises and other users in terms of services and applications.

The key issue in modern telecommunications is the speed and efficiency of information transmission. The big impacts of telecommunications upon the efficient functioning of enterprises have been improvement in transmission speeds and in particular new methods of enhancing the movement of information. They have been complemented by reductions in memory cost, enhanced video processing power and innovations in software. Traditionally, telecommunications were based upon copper wire which moved information by sound waves. The move to fibre optic cable (based on light transmission), which occupies the same space, means that information can be carried 100,000 times faster.[24] Much of the impact of the information revolution will be dependent on the installation of fibre optic cable into the entire network. Of growing importance is the increased sophistication of access tools. Mass access to networks is increasingly sensitive to the price of related equipment. Other notable trends are the rise of integration (where a number of services are delivered over a single point of access) and universal interoperability of networks. Such developments in combination will be powerful forces driving network technology on a global basis.

Information technology (IT) is an essential complement to advanced telecommunications and central to an economy's ability to access and utilise information to its advantage. IT will define how the information available can be used on a micro level while the existence of telecommunication networks will

11

ensure that this can occur over space. The rates of adoption and penetration of IT are symptomatic of how efficiently an economy is handling information.

The convergence of computing and telecommunications is creating the demand to sustain the roll-out of advanced networks. It is important, however, to guarantee that IT is dispersed to ensure that new technological divides do not emerge. Growing global economic constraints are putting pressure on IT suppliers in line with the telecommunications network to supply greater functionality (Monk 1992).[25] Such a trend indicates that the telecommunications policy is too narrow; the focus should be upon an information policy (Macdonald 1992).[26]

NATURE OF TENS IN TELECOMMUNICATIONS

The essence of trans-European telecommunication networks (telecom-TENs) is to seek the sustained roll-out of advanced networks and associated technology in an interoperable and interconnected fashion. In short, if these networks are to complement the development of the information society, they should be spatially and socially non-discriminatory. It is important to underline that telecom-TENs are not about the establishment of a single all-embracing network but the development of a series of networks that are integrated to an extent that each represents a subsystem of the larger network.

The aim is to promote the roll-out and introduction of narrowband (E-ISDN) and broadband (IBC) networks[27] across the EU, ensuring that they are offered to all sizes of enterprises and eventually to the mass residential market. It is important that the evolution of networks from narrowband to broadband is plotted, which in practice means the gradual shift from ISDN towards IBC over time (see Table 1.2). Networks are likely to evolve that deliver the functionality required of them as users become more technologically sophisticated.

Under the powers given to the Commission via article 129c of the Treaty upon European Union, the Community aims to establish a series of guidelines for projects that are deemed to be of common interest. While short on specific projects, these must be specified by users under the call for proposals which happen thereafter. It is hoped that the series of guidelines should lead to the deployment of an advanced communications infrastructure throughout the EU by the end of the first two decades of the next millennium.

Inevitably the successful development of these networks will be based upon the TENs criteria (see below) while satisfying user requirements and meeting the broader economic and industrial concerns that are inherent within the development of these networks. Officially a trans-European telecommunication network has three layers:[28]

1 Applications: these enable the average end user to access the advanced networks and in practice represent the focal point of network development.

In short, the development of applications is about practical utilisation of information and communication.

2 Generic services: while applications tend to be sector specific, these services tend to be applicable across a range of users. Hence their use can be encouraged as broadly as possible. It is hoped that services such as E-mail and file transfer will become more widely used throughout the socio-economic structures.

3 Basic networks: these are the means via which users will access the services and thus provide mass delivery channels. Ensuring that these networks provide integrated service functions as well as reflecting the rapidity of technological change is a key objective.

The pattern for the development of telecom-TENs (as reflected in Figure 1.1) underlines the importance of applications as the foundation stone for the development of networks.[29] The establishment of a clear user need for applications is likely to be the basis for the development of services and the profitable roll-out of advanced integrated infrastructure. Thus, the success of advanced networking depends upon the network provider being able to satisfy real user demands. This is important given the user-led nature of the development of the information society.

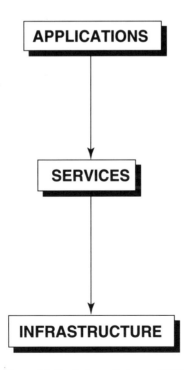

Figure 1.1 Evolution of telecom-TENs

13

Figure 1.2 Roll-out of advanced networks within user communities

In the user-led scenario for the development of TENs, priorities between users will inevitably be set. Such priorities, which are reflected in the EU's strategy, represent commercial and technical realities of the migration towards advanced telecommunications by differing user groups. Figure 1.2 highlights the schematised proposal for the introduction and development of telecom-TENs within certain user groups. Under a market-led route initial developments will inevitably focus upon the area of the market that is most sensitive to advanced telecommunications: business. Thereafter the desire is to let the market evolve into the professions and eventually into the residential market.

No time span is given for this evolutionary path. Such a market-led strategy will probably require supplement from the public sector. This is likely to occur on both the supply and demand sides of the market to ensure that the concerns of TENs are met. Such public sector action is justified by the perception of the eventual commonality of interest between these user groups in the development of advanced telecommunications. This path evidently represents a route map to the development of the information society.

The user-led nature of these networks means that it is important that the proposals deemed of common interest reflect a clear need upon which sustainable demand and thus network diffusion can be based. Any complementary action by the public sector is likely to be founded upon such criteria. This is important; if the development of TENs is going to contribute to the competitiveness of the EU it has to be in areas where enterprises need improvement and where their competitive position is best enhanced. Networks tend to be most economically viable when they are responding to real needs and requirements.

The capabilities of the networks that are emerging in Europe are initially to be based upon E-ISDN with an osmotic migration to broadband as consumer demands become more sophisticated. This can be schematised into a number of phases which plot the evolution of telecom-TENs (see Table 1.2). In truth it is difficult to say where the network stops evolving. One can only offer a conjecture that once fibre optics are in place throughout the local loop network, evolution will stem more from the application of ICTs which exploit the high capacities offered by this infrastructure.

Table 1.2 The evolution of telecommunications networks

Time Period	Network
1990–2000	Implementation and widespread deployment of E-ISDN
1995–2010	Implementation of TEN-IBC, especially to business users
2000–2010	Integration of mobility and network intelligence
2005–2020	Establishment of photonic network*

Source: European Parliament, 1993
*A photonic network is one where all network functions are derived through fibre optic devices.

If these networks are to aid the competitiveness of the EU they must facilitate action by enterprises which will assist in the broad horizontal objectives of the EU's industrial policy. To achieve this networks must fulfil the criteria of TENs. This is central if the emergence of the network economy is to be realised and if these ICTs and telecommunication networks are to work to the economic advantage of the EU.

THE TENS CRITERIA

The concerns of TENs are reflected in the TENs criteria (see Figure 1.3) which reflect the features that telecommunication networks need to exhibit if they are to contribute directly to the EU's industrial strategy. Title XII of the Treaty upon European Union offers a set of criteria expected from networks if they are to work to the full benefit of the EU. As the Treaty states:

> Within the framework of a system of open and competitive markets, action by the Community shall aim at promoting the interconnection and interoperability of national networks as well as access to such networks. It shall take account in particular of the need to link island, landlocked and peripheral regions with the central regions of the Community.[30]

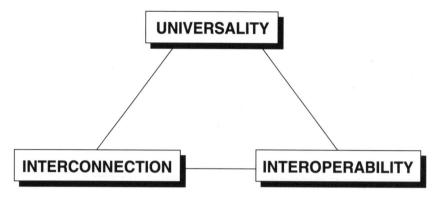

Figure 1.3 The TENs criteria

These concerns contribute to many aspects of the TENs programme, from the development of the information society through to ensuring that regions of the EU share in this new technology. If the telecommunications network is to develop as a true TEN it has to be seen to fulfil these criteria. They do overlap as the concerns of universality run alongside interconnection, just as inter-connection complements the attainment of interoperability. In developing a strategy for the attainment of TENs, the member states and the institutions of the EU need to take account of these criteria.

The development of the TENs criteria in telecommunications is symptomatic of the rise of what Noam (1990) terms the pluralist network, that is a large number of sub-networks derived from a large number of vendors which contributes to an integrated unified network. Thus within an integrated system there is a fair degree of diversity. The idea is to ensure that each of these networks develops in a holistic manner and contributes to broader policy objectives.

Interoperability

This is a historical legacy of the traditional planning of infrastructures at the member state level. In telecommunications this has led to incompatibility of national networks, both in technical and tariffing terms, thereby hindering cross-border communications. The more networks fall into line, the easier it will be for information to flow across borders. The issue for interoperability in tele-communications is vital, not just for the networks themselves but also for the deployment of the equipment associated with this advanced technology. It is necessary to ensure that where ICTs emerge and develop their use is holistic, thus enabling network externalities to be fully exploited (see Chapter 2). The existence of network externalities means that users are likely to buy equipment and develop networks which deliver the greatest functionality. Such functionality is derived from a network that enables the user to access the greatest number of alternative users, a benefit directly derived from the attainment of interoperability.

The issue of compatibility is not only important for the realisation of network externalities but also for ensuring that enterprises can mix and match equipment to enable them to achieve maximum functionality from the network. In a competitive environment the desire to be compatible with the dominant standard is vital to a firm's success. Such issues go hand in hand with interconnection (see below).

The development of interoperability raises clear issues for standardisation bodies at the national and supranational level and for the industry itself. These in turn are central to the complete evolution of the network economy. Generally there needs to be a governmental role in the standardisation process as market-led development would only tend to see standards evolve over a sustained period of time.

Interconnection

Closely linked into the theme of interoperability is that of interconnection. It means in the first instance the physical integration of networks to ensure trans-frontier interoperability. Basic interconnection exists and has done for a number of years in some cases, for example basic telephony. The major challenge is to ensure that an advanced infrastructure emerges in an interconnected fashion to develop, in an integrated manner, the network of networks that is at the heart of TENs in telecommunications. Again the attainment of this objective relies upon a reorientation of national network planning. The needs for interconnection have risen in importance within telecommunications as the process of liberal-isation has advanced. This underlines the fact that each enterprise belongs to a series of networks which need to be interconnected if firms are to communicate effectively. This is important in the multi-operator, multi-vendor environment where different networks are emerging and need to be interconnected. Many of them lack true ubiquity as the ability of the general populous to access them is limited due to specific technology or their limited territorial scope. As a consequence true ubiquity is only achievable by the PTO. Interconnection renders the PTO, in this transition phase, the messenger and common carrier[31] for all other operators to ensure ubiquity of their services is achieved. In turn this interconnection has to work both ways, with the PTO being able to access the network of alternative network suppliers.

Interconnection therefore has important implications in creating the demand for such a network and justifying such investment. The physical integration of separate networks creates enhanced scope for the exploitation of network externalities as it will tend to increase significantly the number of alternative users that are accessible via this network. Consequently, intercon-nection should have positive welfare effects. In truth such interconnections reflect the practical increases in interactions across borders that have resulted from the number of legislative changes, associated with the SEM, across the continent. Both interconnection and its interlinked concept of interoperability are born of the necessary internationalisation of networks that has derived from the greater functionality that enterprises are demanding.

Universality

In terms of policy, universality stresses the importance of access to advanced networks by a wide range of socio-economic groupings irrespective of their physical/geographic location. Universality therefore implies potential and feasible access to the network by all economic groupings and regions. Universality need not mean supplying advanced telecommunications services to all households and SMEs. The attitude taken is to ensure public access, not necessarily via residential services but through some central public location such as a library. Thus universality, initially at least, is focused upon the community rather than the domestic level. Over the medium term this is deemed to be a more cost-effective method of diffusing advanced services throughout the socio-economic space.

Access

Ensuring access to the network is inevitably linked to the attainment of interoperability as well as being part of the successful cohesion concerns of network development. In short, access is integral to the information society and economy achieving its desired effects. This implies that all users and service providers who want to access the network can do so in a non-discriminatory manner.

The ability and desirability of consumers to access these networks requires an increased awareness of their capabilities. Only with this stimulus will the level of sustained demand exist to encourage the full roll-out. These issues are also important in ensuring the shifting goal of universal access. Since the strategy for the development of networks is to be market led, the potential denial of access to vulnerable groups and areas emerges. The public service element of these networks cannot be divorced completely from their commercial provision. Without universal service the full benefits of the shift to the information society will tend to be dissipated. Wider access by services providers should not preclude wider access by the general populous. Universal service means equal treatment in terms of types of service that can be accessed and tariffs at which they are available. The need to maintain this broad access is important as changes in the nature of supply have meant that greater value added is derived from the network as users have become more sophisticated.

There is a need to differentiate between access and consumption (Olsen and Rogers 1991). Clearly there is a difference between providing access to the network and the actual consumption of services. In the development of TENs the two are interrelated. If network development is to deliver the anticipated benefits, the services which are now accessible need to be consumed. Consumption represents the demand for the network. Commercial operators will have little incentive to offer access if it is not utilised. A direct legacy for policy is that access and schemes to encourage consumption need to co-ordinate in the development of telecom-TENs.

Cohesion

Promoting economic and social cohesion is one of the central planks of the competitiveness strategy of the EU. The application of ICTs should help regional development due to time–space and cost–space convergence. These factors should promote greater centrafugalism in economic development as the physical remoteness of areas is less of a disadvantage. If these factors are to work to reduce cost pressure upon the core and ensure more evenly decentralised growth, then the infrastructure has to be developed in these regional areas. Therefore any strategy for the development of TENs has to consider the regional dimension of these networks if they are to complement the development of the EU. True mobility and access will only be achieved if networks are developed evenly in an interconnected and interoperable fashion across all economic operators and potential users in all parts of the area. This is a particular challenge for the strategy given lower levels of network development and penetration in the periphery and the consequent need for large sustained investment if it is not to fall further behind the core. Consequently TENs are seen as a binding force in the economic development of Europe.

The criteria within TENs are designed to aid and respond to the market-led development of these networks. Interoperability, interconnection and certain forms of access will all be pro-active in leading the commercial development of networks. Cohesion and universal access concerns are designed to counter the less positive side of market-led development. As a result, policy-based stimuli to help the demand for ICTs and telecommunication networks seek to aid the commercial development of TENs. The EU is pushing to establish an integrated telecommunication system by promoting standardised networks and even availability of services to ensure the harmonious advance of future networks development. Actions on the supply side of the telecommunications market are only one aspect of policy. The EU also needs to be concerned with demand-creating devices if commercial investment for telecom-TENs is to be forthcoming.

CONCLUSION

As mentioned above, policy is geared to aiding market-induced change rather than seeking to work against it. The issue to be argued is that the themes within TENs reflect these broad policy concerns and that any elements of activism, whether by the states or the EU, are responsive to such changes.

The TENs criteria outline what a network has to be if it is to complement fully all the concerns within the EU's industrial strategy. The aim is to investigate how far the strategy and specific networks meet these criteria and whether those being developed commercially are true TENs or just advancements in European infrastructure. The issue here is that TENs are a motor of integration born out of the freer interplay of markets and not from any grand political scheme. In short, markets not politics create the need for TENs and the criteria which define them.

A market-led strategy requires that private investment leads infrastructure investment. The issue to be examined is the extent to which that investment is compatible with the TENs criteria. Within a market framework, the role of the EU as an actor needs to be explored. The theme here is that market failure requires the EU to be active in managing networks so that the TENs criteria are fulfilled. In the light of such features the impact of information and tele-communications needs to be more fully appreciated.

2

TELECOMMUNICATIONS, INDUSTRIAL COMPETITIVENESS AND THE EMERGING NETWORK ECONOMY

INTRODUCTION

The previous chapter highlighted the role of advanced communications within the EU's industrial competitiveness strategy. It highlighted the features that telecom-TENs need to exhibit if they are to complement the EU's industrial policy objectives. This chapter aims to examine why it is important for networks to exhibit these features by understanding their positive impact upon enterprise performance within both European and global theatres.

In many senses information can be seen as the fifth freedom alongside those allowed by the development of the SEM. As firms internationalise, so the importance increases of movements of information and advanced telecommunications across borders, as a means of allocating resources in an efficient manner. This in part explains the prominence given to the Common Information Area (CIA). For the network to aid enterprises to exploit the freedoms facilitated by the SEM, they need to develop as TENs. If networks do not develop in an integrated manner firms will find that their internationalisation strategies are increasingly frustrated. Consequently, these networks can be seen as a direct complement to the strengthening of the competitive position of Europe's enterprises.

This chapter seeks to demonstrate how and in what ways advanced telecommunications will facilitate an improved competitive performance, both on a micro- and macro-economic basis. This is examined from two key perspectives:

- The importance of the physical infrastructures within the emergence of the network economy; the development of this form of organisation is a direct response to the freedoms created by the SEM which need to be supported by advanced telecommunications networks.
- The importance of information and communications technologies in meeting the broad industrial competitiveness objectives of the EU.

21

INFORMATION AND THE SINGLE MARKET: THE EMERGING NETWORK ECONOMY

The opening of markets and the freer mobility of factors of production have led to strategic responses by enterprises across space. Whether reflected in terms of inter-firm relationships or intra-firm reorganisations, such responses need to be underpinned by the provision of physical infrastructure. The emergence of such relationships has led to alterations in the demand for advanced telecommunications to support the increased spatial dimension of an enterprise's functioning.

It is important to underline that the physical infrastructure acts as a facilitator of such changes and is not a cause in its own right. Infrastructure may be provided but the competitive benefits will only be felt when its potentialities are exploited by operators. Such factors underpin the economic importance of network infrastructures that exhibit the features of interconnection, interoperability and universality as a means of supporting the economic activities of enterprises. Within the context of the emerging network economy, infrastructure is merely the physical means for the mass delivery of value creating services.

The network economy is a rising form of industrial organisation in the late twentieth century. The essence of a network economy is one in which the major form of wealth and value creation stems from a series of architectures that facilitate the combined management of a whole series of individual relationships (Bressand and Nicolaidis 1990). The rise of the network economy is indicative of the rise of intra-industry trade, co-operation in terms of research and development[1] and the rise of trans-national enterprises. The rise of the network economy can be accounted for by, first, the rising intensity and complexity of human interactions; second, a reduction in the importance of geographical territory as a determination of accessibility; third, the failure of the market to solve inter-firm relations in an increasingly complex economic environment.

The network economy is basically a series of tangible (infrastructure) and intangible (inter-relationships) interlinkages between or within enterprises operating within the global economy. Consequently the network becomes central to the efficient functioning of the enterprise, which means that maintenance of the network is of increasing commercial importance. Batten (1991)[2] perceives the network economy as exhibiting the following characteristics:

- economic activities serving or located within a set of specific places called nodes (economic operators);
- a series of links that connect these nodes (infrastructure);
- a large number of flows across these links between the respective nodes (services).

The industrial system is comprised of a network of operators engaged in production, distribution and use of commodities. This is based upon a series of inter-relationships between enterprises where each operator functions in a niche within a defined network. The division of work in the network creates a series of interdependencies that are inherently different from other aspects of market development (Johanson and Mattsson 1988). Networks increasingly represent a form of economic organisation through which agents deal as the production process becomes ever more information intensive.[3] As this process exhibits greater pertinence so the need for better and faster physical links emerges as an expression of mutual interest.

Physical networks have to provide flexibility in response to the changing needs of the enterprise. Consequently network management becomes a key tool of enterprise functioning. A firm must continually appraise its network, its place in it and its capabilities to ensure that it works to its economic advantage. This includes not only the series of inter-relationships with which it is involved but also the quality of the infrastructure which supports its actions. Ultimately the market place, according to this perspective, will be characterised by a series of networks between different types of firm. The interdependence between enterprises is such that the activities of one firm depend upon the effective utilisation of resources by another. As a result no enterprise can be understood in isolation and without reference to its relationships with other firms (Thorelli 1986). Networks therefore need to be seen as a strategic tool that enables firms to position themselves in the market (Jarillo 1988).

This will inevitably be complemented by the development and deployment of information and communication systems, a fact underlined by their increasingly prominent impact upon enterprise functioning (see below). This is altering rapidly, together with the general environment of enterprises. These developments have profound effects upon the economic environment as interaction and improved technology remove the salience of geography in the location decision. As a consequence the network economy represents an opportunity to operate production across a more geographically dispersed system. Such systems are indicative of changing production patterns as the shift towards just-in-time techniques replaces the perceived antiquities of Fordism. The shift to these new production techniques relies upon fast and exact communication systems and increasingly efficient and effective information handling. Organisationally the rise of the network economy facilitates the rise of transnational enterprises (TNEs) that exploit the 'new international division of labour' within the production process.

Across a broader perspective the move from economies of scale to mass customisation removes the emphasis from large-scale production as a means of achieving efficiency to the linking of operators in such a manner as to reduce the costs of production (Bressand and Nicolaidis 1990). Networks are an organisational response to these desires. Whether inter- or intra-firm, such organisational responses aim to share risk, rationalise upon transaction costs and encourage more efficient production.

Networking strategies of enterprises are increasingly focused on meeting global information requirements (Mansell 1994). Firms that are able to integrate advanced communication services within their overall business strategy are perceived to have a greater likelihood of attaining a sustainable competitive advantage (Mansell and Jenkins 1992).[4] As the nature of production becomes increasingly transnational, so there is the shift towards the network enterprise as a model for firms within the global marketplace. Ideally the networked enterprise will, in terms of telecommunications, combine public and private network options to produce the optimum configuration for its communication needs. As the network starts to become an important economic resource so political pressure on the authorities grows to create an environment conducive to meeting these information requirements; that is an economic need creates political pressure to change the regulatory environment. A particular area of dissatisfaction is the comparative absence of high-speed data communications links. The competitive environment is the means to promote infrastructure investment which goes to the heart of the strategy to develop a new high-speed telecommunications network (see Chapter 3).

The fragmentation of existing networks has tended to inflate the cost of corporate telecommunications services relative to Europe's major competitors.[5] The inflated cost of inter- and intra-firm communications is likely to be a significant hurdle to the fuller exploitation of the Single European Market (SEM), especially to small and medium-sized enterprises (SMEs) for whom the inability to have free flows of communication across borders represents a potentially significant hurdle to their development. Most large enterprises can use their leverage and develop a private/public network configuration that meets their needs more completely. The nature of the information economy is such that telecommunication networks are a vital resource for all economic operators, no matter what size. To enable a response to this demand the EU is in the process of expanding the SEM principles to the telecommunications sector.[6]

The shift towards the network economy creates the need to render inter-operable and increasingly interconnectable the information networks of EU states. While some degree of interconnection and interoperability has existed for some time, it was limited to rudimentary forms of communications (i.e. basic forms of voice and data). The degree of internationalisation of networks was also limited in terms of its coverage. The result was that the capability of networks to meet the information requirements of operators in the network economy was seriously curtailed.

The changes upon enterprises wrought by the development of the network economy have altered the business demands for communication products and services in a number of key ways. Norton (1990) puts this demand into three distinct classes:

- the demand for the better use of facilities such as private networks based upon leased lines;
- the demand for better infrastructure;
- the demand for applications that give clear competitive advantage.

Each of these is derived from the information and communication requirements of enterprises within the network economy. The users want the network to have sufficient physical capabilities that such developments can improve the performance of the enterprise relative to its competitors. If the physical network cannot handle the quantity and quality of interactions derived from the network economy then it will dissipate its economic effects.

Overall telecommunications have to be an integral part of the global network firm. Policy has to seek to influence and ensure that the network delivers all that is expected. While such pressures devolve on suppliers, it is up to regulatory bodies to ensure that such opportunities exist. The network as a true business resource will ultimately be determined by the rules that govern its operation. As such regulatory bodies have to supplement market forces and not seek to retard them.

The legacy of the rise of the network economy for policy-makers is manifold. Jacquemin and Marchipont (1993) indicate that its development creates an increasingly narrow interdependence, rendering the means of influencing industrial structures more complex; as a result the 'terms of reference for government . . . and the terms of efficiency of economic operators are increasingly out of step'.[7] The establishment of these networks means that the effects of policy become increasingly difficult to predict as domination and its effects become more complex. As Jacquemin and Sapir (1990) indicate, the economic interest of an area becomes harder to define, especially in an environment where the level of agreement and network establishment tends to render the spheres of influence of states increasingly fuzzy.

The network economy is now seen as the source of value creation within modern economies. This poses a number of issues for the development of industrial policy. Policy seeks to determine and manage the realisation of physical infrastructures and the economic inter-relationships that occur over them. But actions are also likely to influence the form and nature of such interactions. As firms reorganise themselves internationally and new inter-relationships are formed, there needs be vigilance by bodies to ensure that the catalysts of industrial competitiveness are not undermined. Such vigilance should not allow value from these networks to be diminished.

While the network is seen as an important economic asset for operators, its effectiveness is limited by the degree of coverage. Firms may wish to be part of the network but resist because its coverage does not deliver the value required. In establishing inter- or intra-firm networks the ability to do so in a particular area will depend upon the reach of the physical network and its accessibility. The more complete the coverage of the network, the greater the value it will potentially provide to its users. This will enable firms to exploit international division of labour and organise themselves more efficiently. In short, the greater the coverage, the greater the value derived.

INDUSTRIAL COMPETITIVENESS AND DEVELOPMENT
OF TELECOM-TENS

The ways in which the development of trans-European telecommunication networks complement the broader objectives of the EU's industrial strategy are manifold. The development of telecommunication networks is likely to increase the salience of information within modern economies. This is enhanced by the growing importance of the network economy in Europe which has further implications in terms of harmonious economic development and regeneration.

Denmead and Ablett (1994) point to a number of reasons why the network has become increasingly central to the enterprise, notably:

- the importance of telecommunications as a means of reorganising and automating business functions;
- increasing commercial pressure globally, creating the desire for faster product evolution and a need to respond quickly to user pressure;
- its effects upon locational decisions, for example where to place the head-quarters, production facilities and distribution centres.

According to Jacquemin and Marchipont (1993) the major contributor to the competitiveness of an economy is investment in human capital as 'this is what determines the long-term ability of economies to stay in the race for industrial and technological competitiveness'. Such an improvement in human capital is a major concern of the moves towards the information society which TENs in telecommunications are designed to underpin (see later). What needs to be established in broad terms is how telecom-TENs, as a 'non-mobile factor', assist competitiveness.

Telecom-TENs are a facilitator of competitiveness; on their own they can do little. The focus has to be on a catalytic role in provoking enterprises to behave in a manner that is in the broader economic interest of the economy. The impact of telecom-TENs is only as good as the quality of the services that are available over them; as such it is only as good as the rights of access and mobility created by a complementary legal and regulatory environment. This underlines that telecom-TENs are a necessary policy initiative to get firms to respond in a desirable way to the freedoms enhanced and created by the SEM. The broad complementarity between industrial policy and telecom-TENs is highlighted in Table 2.1.

The service element of the networks has to be a key factor in their contribution to competitiveness. The effect of telecom-TENs can only be judged to the extent that they meet the requirements of enterprises operating across borders. The services offered must meet the concerns of mobility and accessibility in an effective and efficient manner. These networks should seek to offer better quality services at lower cost to overcome any friction, in terms of distance, that can deter trade and competition. All firms will incur a network cost which amounts to transaction cost. Trading with other parts of the economic space is

Table 2.1 TENs interlinkages with industrial policy

Policy objective	TENs theme
Single market	Assist mobility and accessibility between and within national markets
Improve quality of labour	ICT training and vocational training networks
Increase technological capacity/expertise	Encourage innovation and spread of ICTs
SMEs	Increase access to high quality infrastructure and lower cost of communication services
Develop business services	Increase quality and quantity of network services
Cohesion	Improve network development in peripheral areas
Better organisation of production	Encourage development work of network expertise
Modern role for public authorities	Realise TENs through public/private sector partnerships

not cost free. The establishment of an environment where these transaction costs can be reduced and hopefully minimised, will create the right complementary environment for true interaction across the entire EU. If any part of the network remains underdeveloped the higher transaction cost involved could put this area at a disadvantage. The ability of telecom-TENs to deliver such savings will be a core factor in determining their successful impact upon the commercial environment.

Implicit within the development of telecom-TENs is that the EU must utilise the development of the network economy to its own advantage. The Commission stresses that 'the geographical (national or European) thinking ... must gradually make way for thinking in terms of worldwide networks'.[8] Parochialism in national planning must not be replaced by a similar phenomenon at the European level. Thus the prosperity of the EU relies upon a globalised network of firms obtaining resources worldwide that can contribute to its economic development. Securing diverse supplies from as broad an area as possible ensures that networks are seen as a strategic asset for the entire economic area.

The key is in the better organisation of production and more efficient enterprise functioning across borders. The development of these networks is expected to yield a cost benefit by allowing resources to be allocated more efficiently and effectively and by facilitating lower network costs. In addition the development of these networks allows the wider availability of information essential for market functioning, enabling resources to be more readily available.

The incompleteness of networks in relation to Europe's major competitors currently pushes its economy into a disadvantageous position on the global stage. In particular great store is put in utilising ICTs via telecom-TENs to foster more efficient working practices, thereby increasing productivity and value added. The services provided give the impetus to organise along more efficient lines and to develop a more effective administrative and managerial system.

The economic development of regions has been readily influenced by the provision of infrastructure. In terms of the core–periphery dichotomy, the role of TENs is to reduce, in temporal terms, distance and physical remoteness. In this case industrial policy themes are inevitably intertwined with the broader processes of economic convergence within the EU. Hence within the grand plans for EMU, telecom-TENs have a distinct role. They need to ensure that markets work effectively and that the entire area can operate as an economic unit. The centripetal effects of economic integration must not hinder such progress. The emerging network economy and its associated effects therefore have a political role to play. There appears to be little incentive for peripheral states to subscribe to a process that will inevitably work to their disadvantage.

Consequently, insofar as the strategy to achieve telecom-TENs includes elements of activism, it is in the provision of an advanced and highly developed infrastructure across as broad a geographical plane as possible. Such action is based again upon the logic of the market and how best the future competitiveness of the EU can be attained. Policy of the EU pertains that such centralisation represents 'a potential economic loss'.[9] As a result 'future competitiveness must rely less upon economies of scale and large series and more upon the capacity to assimilate information and to ensure its appropriate dissemination, thereby offering the possibility of decentralised industrial growth'.[10] This underlines that the prolonged interlinkages between industrial competitiveness and cohesion rely upon using the regions as a means to sustain growth and competitiveness in the EU when the core becomes congested. For these reasons there is believed to be a strong link between cohesion and industrial competitiveness (CEC 1994a). The success of these regions must be modelled upon the economic strength of the core. Increasingly this has to be information-led, offering the possibility of high value added industries being created. In a global network economy the underprovision of infrastructure would work to the detriment of EU economic integration and unification.

Competitive advantage through the development of telecom-TENs can also be derived from the existence of network externalities, which are prevalent within telecommunication networks (see Chapter 3). According to Capello (1994) network externalities provide a micro-stimulus which breeds a micro-response, in terms of the performance of enterprises, and a macro-response thereafter as regional economic performance is enhanced. The establishment of networks creates the possibility of their own dynamism which feeds through into the broader diffusion of information, communication and best practice.

The basis of this enhanced economic performance is gleamed from 'economic symbiosis'[11] which is 'an improvement in economic performance based upon non-paid-for synergies among firms'.[12] A group of enterprises connected via a common physical network gains productivity advantages over non-networked

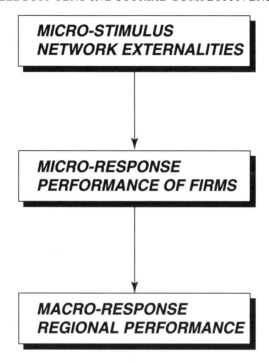

Figure 2.1 A framework for network externality effects
Source: Capello, 1994

firms in both static terms (via better synergies and information provision) and dynamic terms (via complementary assets, greater network based innovation and entering previously unknown markets).

The importance of these synergetic and symbiotic effects relies upon the fact that the marginal price for achieving such benefits is non-existent. As a result technical and pecuniary externalities can be exploited which according to Capello (1994) means that networked firms are capable of generating dynamic growth via spillover and multiplier effects. This analysis is simplistic and only focuses upon one element influencing the performance of an enterprise. The positive externality effects are likely to occur in the case of exclusive networks, where there is the possibility of discriminating between members, non-members and, importantly for the case of telecom-TENs, the public network. In the latter case, the benefits are not based upon a voluntary decision but upon how the network and the technologies available are used by the firm or group of firms to their own economic advantage. This is important for simply being connected to a network does not mean that the economic advantages are automatic. As Capello (1994) indicates, benefits are derived from the economic interest upon which connectivity is based, not upon simply being a member of the network.

These symbiotic effects can be exploited for the purposes of regional development if networked firms are clustered in a geographically defined area. This produces agglomeration economies derived from the networking process.[13] In simple terms the interlinkage of network firms on an inter- or intra-regional basis can lead to exchanges of know-how, information and better methods of production. On a broad level these advantages will be achieved by ensuring the dispersal of information, expanding geographical markets, gaining new specialised factor inputs and obtaining specialised knowledge from other areas. The exploitation of these opportunities is greatest where there is a highly developed infrastructure, a large number of innovative firms and an 'advanced' labour market.

Traditional thinking states that the aforementioned time–space and cost–space convergence promoted by ICTs should promote more even regional development (Janelle 1991). According to Capello (1994) the application of ICTs upon spatial development is by no means certain. It is feasible that technological diffusion is a centripetal process so the development of ICTs would increase regional disadvantage. Such disadvantages rise from lower levels of users, lower effectiveness of network externalities and reduced capability to achieve a critical mass in the adoption process. The denial of access to networks by peripheral areas is obviously going to present a competitiveness and industrial strategy problem. The provision of telecommunications infrastructure *per se* is not good enough. What needs to be encouraged is their innovative use and the type of information that is delivered. The strategists would need to develop the right policy to realise such applications. These tendencies have already been noted in the plans for the information society.

Any benefits from the development of telecom-TENs have to be established in the light of network costs, which are by no means static. The relative marginal costs and benefits of network participation will determine where and to what extent it is used. It is evident that benefits can be obtained from a network at both the firm and regional level. However, this may be countered by network congestion, externalities and free riders. If a region develops a network it may only increase the competitiveness of a rival region. For example, the development of telecom-TENs could result in central and Eastern Europe being a more attractive arena for investment. As a consequence the region being networked must already have some potential for economic development. Therefore network development does not yield benefits as a matter of course.

The institutional framework within which ICTs are introduced is fundamental to ensuring that they have the desired competitive effects. Forcing the pace of change may offer little benefit as staff may be untrained and resistant to change and the equipment may operate to old standards (Mansell 1995; Teece 1995).[14] Such conditions will tend to negate any productivity effects felt from the broad adoption of these technologies. The resources required for training and equipment imply that the adoption of ICTs will vary both between and within sectors. The process of adoption cannot be forced; it has to be a result of a decision at the micro level, taken on a firm by firm basis.

Early adopters of technology may benefit from establishing a market niche but would tend to exhibit the highest costs of adjustment. Such effects would be felt in terms of purchasing and installing the initial forms of the technology as well as burdening the uncertainties surrounding the adoption of a new technology. Those that follow would tend to get round such problems but may suffer due to the lack of first starter advantage.

A recent survey has indicated the substantial benefits to be obtained from the development of an advanced telecommunications infrastructure.[15] Over the period 1993–2008 the development of advanced communication systems will add between 2.7 and 6 per cent to the EU's GDP growth rate.[16] Many of these benefits will be felt most in the core regions of Europe. Further studies have also indicated the advantages of the development of advanced information infrastructures. A report to the US government stated that for every dollar invested in infrastructure there are anticipated gains of 1.6 dollars to GDP.[17] This is supported by a recent report published in France which suggested that the expenditure upon networks could result in a tripling of activity in related services with a substantial impact upon employment.[18]

One of the notable changes in the European economy is the shift towards information intensive activities. Such a trend is important given the trend towards a more capital intensive manufacturing sector, which is likely to concentrate on high technology products as the developing world undertakes those tasks that are more labour intensive.[19] If the information revolution is to work to the competitive advantage of the EU it has to penetrate all socio-economic structures of the EU to ensure that the economy can respond flexibly to the pressures exerted upon it.

The improvements to productivity envisaged by the application of ICTs are seen as a precursor of competitiveness and sustained economic growth. These ICTs are also important in enabling enterprises to adapt to change by introducing new methods of organisation as the economy moves towards pro-ductive techniques, based upon immaterial production methods driven by the importance of information. Despite global changes, manufacturing is still likely to remain important to the European economy. What will change is the type of production and how it is produced. As labour intensive manufacturing shifts elsewhere, the emphasis will be upon establishing high technology sectors to exploit the intellectual content of industry, thus aiding its productivity.

Confland (1993) identifies four levels of competitiveness that are closely linked to information which all tend to be sustainable:

1 The reinforcement of strategic vision and means of assisting decision-making: greater uncertainty that results from globalisation requires new forms of strategic methods; better information reduces uncertainty by creating better knowledge about the economic environment.

2 The rationalisation and optimisation of production: the effectiveness of trade depends upon the ability of information technology to link up clients with

producers, develop just-in-time production methods and enable greater flexibility in the production and design of goods to meet more completely the ever changing needs of the market.

3 The increase in the reactivity and flexibility of organisations: in a rapidly changing economic environment the enterprise needs to respond quickly to changes.

4 The development of technology and innovation: information provides the means for firms to innovate in response to the dynamics of the market; it is also the means via which best practice and new technology reach into the broader economic sphere.

In turn these factors depend upon four 'facilitating factors' (Confland 1993):

- the mastery of uncertainty;
- the substitution of a functional approach with a product based approach;
- the promotion of human resources and intellectual investment;
- the development of information technologies.

The impact of these factors means that information in whatever form is central to an enterprise understanding the economic environment in which it works. Whether this information is in the form of market research or databases it provides the means upon which business can make decisions. The more information that an enterprise has in its possession, the lower the degree of risk it faces in any investment or commercial decision. Once the importance of information has been established, the emphasis is then placed upon using it to assist competitive advantage. The role of ICTs, networks and labour trained in the utilisation of information is paramount. The information that a firm possesses is only as good as its ability to utilise it effectively. The more people that have access to the information across a broader space, the better the economy performs. Information has no intrinsic value; it only becomes a true resource when set within the functionality of the enterprise and, increasingly, the economy as a whole.

Gillespe (1987)[20] has indicated on a micro-economic level what the impact of the development of the information economy is likely to be upon the competitive strategies of economic operators. Broadly his conclusions are sixfold:

- product innovation: the emergence of the information economy will give rise to commodities that are transferable over the telecommunications network;
- distribution innovation: where the key information element of goods is more easily distributed throughout the economy;
- production process innovation: the development of advanced communications systems allows for the integration of several automated processes under a single system;
- production process decomposition: this arises due to the belief that it is no longer necessary to locate capital and labour within close proximity;

- transactional innovation: the means via which members of the value chain communicate will be radically altered;
- managerial innovation: the information economy will facilitate the physical separation of activity location and control.

The implementation of these factors within the competitive strategies of enterprises are likely to have a broader macro-economic effect. First, there is likely to be an increase in demand for the products developed by the ICT sector. Second, a technology effect is anticipated as the development of advanced communication systems is likely to lead to a virtuous cycle of technological innovation. Third, a productivity effect is anticipated due to improvements in information handling derived from advancements in infrastructure.

There is little evidence that the application of ICTs is having an impact upon productivity. Most productivity boosts are still believed to be caused by increased inputs of capital and labour.[21] The reasons why ICTs have failed to deliver such productivity gains are disputed. Perhaps the ICT revolution has been overstated and the technology is simply not productive.[22] Investment in ICTs is not always made as a means to boost productivity. Alternatively the anticipated productivity gains have not been realised because ICT use is still in an embryonic phase throughout enterprises. Once they start to comprehend fully the potential of ICTs then benefits should begin to be realised.

Despite such an apparent productivity paradox it is perhaps evident that economies are still in the embryonic phase of the information revolution where the stock of ICTs are too small to make a vast difference to an economy's performance. Productivity gains by ICTs may in fact be difficult to measure. This may offer the most pervasive explanation as to why the anticipated effects of ICTs have not shown through. Many of the gains to the economy are likely to be derived from the service sector, a domain which is notoriously difficult to measure in terms of productivity.

The effect of the application of ICTs upon employment is difficult to assess. The EU clearly believes that if all opportunities are exploited then it should have a positive effect upon employment. However, technical change tends to create a net loss of jobs in the short term with a return to normal values over the longer term (Nickell 1995).[23] The links between more information intensive activities and structural unemployment are as yet unclear.

CONCLUSION

The development of advanced telecommunication networks within the EU is expected to deliver large benefits to the economy. These are likely to accrue at both a micro- and macro-economic level. The network economy and the importance given to information within its realisation are likely to prove pivotal in the realisation of the EU's stated industrial strategy objectives.

A feature of the EU economy has been the increased importance of information to the determination of competitiveness. What is important is that information does not automatically offer benefits. Any positive effect depends upon how firms respond to the opportunities and challenges created by its increased prominence. An important consequence has been the rise in importance of the network economy.

Networks are proving to be powerful factors in the realisation of the objectives of the EU's market-led industrial strategy. The network environment will be broadly market determined. However, this does not preclude a strategy by regulatory bodies to ensure that all types and forms of networks operate in the common interest, i.e. the competitiveness of the economies involved.

3

THE STRATEGY AND INDUSTRIAL FRAMEWORK FOR TRANS-EUROPEAN TELECOMMUNICATION NETWORKS

INTRODUCTION

The previous chapter highlighted the potential economic importance of ICTs for the European economy. Consequently the development of a strategy for telecommunication networks is likely to play a pivotal part in the industrial competitiveness strategy of the EU. The EU is pursuing a market-led approach with a set of initiatives that is designed to combat areas of potential market failure in network development. The criteria set out within the TENs initiative imply the development of a set of integrated networks stretching into all parts of the European economic and social strata, thereby complementing its broad objectives for industrial competitiveness and development. This will need to be complemented by affordable telecommunications, user-led deployment and development strategies, the establishment of a service mentality and activist measures to close Europe's technology gap with the USA and Japan.[1]

This chapter seeks to outline the strategy to develop an advanced telecommunications infrastructure along the lines envisaged within the TENs criteria. The strategy is in effect a two-track approach. One line of policy focuses upon liberalisation as a means of stimulating the desired levels of investment in advanced infrastructures. The second track is the encouragement of collaboration,[2] at competitive and pre-competitive stages, to facilitate the development of these networks as TENs. This twin-track approach seeks to harness both of these forces to develop these networks as broad complements to Europe's industrial policy objectives. In no small part the establishment of such a role is derived from the difference between developing these networks as a concern of policy and their evolution as commercial phenomena.

RATIONALE FOR POLICY DEVELOPMENT

The application of a public sector led strategy to develop TENs is born of the perception or likelihood of the market's inability to deliver TENs in the desired manner. Within the context of the EU's industrial competitiveness objectives, this strategy is based upon first overcoming market failures which deter operator involvement in network development; second, ensuring that markets deliver the desired level and rate of technological change. Thus despite the centre of the EU's strategy for TENs being based upon markets, there is a belief that its extremes need to be controlled. As the market is liberalised, the causes and consequences of market failure are likely to become ever more apparent.

In terms of telecom-TENs, market success or failure is set within the context of attaining the TENs criteria set out within the Treaty upon European Union. These criteria are seen by policy-makers as the central characteristics that networks must exhibit if they are to complement the broad policy themes of the EU's industrial strategy. While the EU sees the market as the desired route, it recognises that it has limits. The 'best' scenario is therefore defined by policy-makers and planners and not by the interaction of market forces.

The nature of market failure that surrounds network development warrants a text on its own. The major potential market failures (some of which are evidently contradictory) include:

- the preservation or re-emergence of monopolistic structures that have the effect of holding back network investment by potential entrant;
- the development of market structures that inhibit the attainment of interconnection and interoperability;
- a degree of competition that increases commercial uncertainty to an extent that it deters investments in network infrastructure;
- informational problems may mean that users and enterprises are poorly informed about economic and social trends, thus retarding technological development;
- underinvestment in supporting structures such as training and education systems;
- the exclusion of certain key socio-economic groups from the information society;
- excessive standardisation as a consequence of commercial action could lower welfare as variety of services etc. is lowered;
- excessive standardisation could also lead to technological inertia which could limit technological development;
- markets could lead to the adoption of an inferior standard that could work to the detriment of the user over the longer term;
- markets may fail to produce a set of agreed standards leading to a process of wasteful competition between rival companies and also limiting the exploitation of network externalities;
- risks and uncertainties involved in developing new technology may limit the

realisation of network externalities and critical mass, therefore retarding network deployment and diffusion.

These failures are indicative of markets and highlight the major potential concerns of policy. They reflect the dangers that could emerge from unregulated or excessive competition. Naturally such concerns do not suggest that reasserting control by the state is justifiable. Many of these failures could just as well occur under this form of control. What is highlighted is that within the chosen strategy potential limitations to its effectiveness are evident.

According to Hall (1986) policy should seek to go to the cause of failure if such phenomena are avoidable and correctable. Developing a common perspective upon how to deal with such failures can and has proved troublesome. States have tended to differ markedly in terms of policy solutions. There are differences concerning the preferred level of intervention between the states. In addition, states also differ upon whether technological development should be part of the planning process or generic economic policy.

The network management role that is the basis of the EU's action is derived from concerns about market failure. This role stresses the need to manage and integrate, within the development of TENs, the apparent contradictory themes of competition and collaboration to ensure the realisation of telecom-TENs in the desired manner. Both of these aspects reflect different concerns related to market failure. Their co-existence is important for each is central to the process of realising telecom-TENs.

In the light of this perspective, the development of the network management role is to address two key concerns:

- to manage the development of telecommunication networks to broadly meet the TENs criteria and overcome any potential market failures in the attainment of these objectives;
- to place the emphasis on the management of inter-firm networks, within which much of the development of telecom-TENs is occurring, to ensure that these directly complement the realisation of telecom-TENs.

Europe's industrial strategy perceives supranational intervention as a necessary catalyst to assist the process of market-provoked structural adjustment. These catalysts involve not only the reregulation of the sector, but also the development of a series of marketable applications. Public sector support is often required in the latter case to push critical mass attainment, to realise the required investment and to overcome uncertainties associated with new technologies. This action has to go beyond telecommunications to the labour market, ensuring that this sector of the economy responds to these structural changes.

Policy measures should seek to pursue an adoption path that does not run beyond the commercial aspirations of enterprises. This is important for the public sector; giving excessive momentum to the process creates the risk of replacing market failure with government failure. Policy is framed within the context of the market. Not understanding the processes could do more harm than good to Europe's competitive position. Policy-makers are not immune from the informational deficiencies that limit market effectiveness as these preferences may also be prone to capture by large players or may simply reflect their own misplaced priorities.

DYNAMICS OF TELECOMMUNICATION NETWORKS AND POLICY IMPLICATIONS

The existence of market failures offers one rationale for the development of policy. Another is linked to the dynamics of network development. Very often policy seeks to utilise these dynamics to push the market for the technology and thus create a virtuous cycle of network deployment and development. However, such dynamics can also work to inhibit network development and deny the onset of technological change.

Any successful market-led route for the development of telecom-TENs is underpinned by the existence of network externalities and its implications for the network attaining critical mass. Network externalities (Katz and Shapiro 1985) reflect the dynamic nature of network development and are derived from the welfare changes, broadly independent of the price mechanism, attached to alterations in the number of users. They are likely to be important in shaping the commercial migration to advanced infrastructure and driving the demand for associated services/applications.

The concept of critical mass and its attainment is directly linked to network externalities. Critical mass is the point at which the network reaches a certain size after which it takes on its own momentum in terms of roll-out, thereby divorcing itself from the need for public sector support. The attainment of critical mass is that level of market size which will allow producers to exploit economies of scale and encourage users to adopt the new technology without any provocation (Allen 1988). According to Stehmann (1995) the concept of critical mass combines both demand (network externalities) and supply side effects (economies of scale and scope). Network externalities underline that a subscriber will only join a network if there is a minimum number of other users. Generally, the more users there are, the more a subscriber is willing to pay to be part of the network. To overcome any inertia associated with a low subscriber pool, low prices may have to be offered until critical mass is achieved. Here price no longer offers the greater incentive for network subscription. Thus if economies of scale are evident, the average cost of the network falls as it takes on its own dynamism (Allen 1988).

At low levels of usage the critical mass will have its own inertia, thus limiting broad network deployment. If the critical mass group is small relative to society, such arguments are not important for the minimum level of users should be easier to achieve. If it is large, it would be very difficult to imagine the sustained market led roll-out of the network. Allen (1988) uses this form of market failure to justify assorted actions such as subsidies or other demand-inducing action to stimulate the realisation of critical mass.

The initial uncertainty of networks, especially where there is unpredictable demand, may require some form of public support for any losses that may occur during the initial stages of network deployment.[3] Such losses may be prohibitive (Stehmann 1995) to network development. These factors have persuaded some states to limit, for a transitional period, the intensity of competition faced by network deployers. However, Stehmann argues that 'the state should refrain from providing the service (given it faces similar risks with no better information) if the private sector does not provide it' (ibid., 52). He qualifies this by indicating that any assistance is only valid where social or political goals are present, which, arguably in the case of the development of the information society, they are.

The role of network externalities in network diffusion indicates that telecom-TENs would have a positive welfare effect upon network users. A large common network which is interconnected, interoperable and physically expanding is likely to deliver greater functionality to users, due to the larger subscriber base, than one that is purely nationally orientated. As each network expands, given a general trend towards economic integration, a greater premium is placed upon each state to interconnect itself as greater economic benefits will be derived. Therefore promoting access is a key factor in enhancing network roll-out.

EVOLVING POLICY TOWARDS TELECOMMUNICATIONS

As a strategy developer, the usefulness of the EU is frequently in the provision of an expression of common concerns and themes and, via its budget, impetus to the process. Its relative financial impotence and dependence upon the goodwill of member states for regulatory effectiveness means that it is at its most effective in setting a common framework and agenda for network development and deployment. It is around this power that policy towards networks has developed.

While it is argued that the *White Paper upon Growth, Competitiveness and Employment* (CEC 1993b) offers 'the closest thing to a broad brush manifesto for telecommunications development policy',[4] action in this area has taken a piecemeal approach for over a decade. A key feature of the industrial strategy involved in the development of telecom-TENs is the establishment of public–private partnerships (PPPs). This strategy allows the development of agreements which bring to the partnership differing expertise and priorities. Such partnerships allow for a distinct division of labour and risk to be formed between the respective sectors as each seeks to attain its own concerns.

Telecommunications policy ultimately stresses the key themes of integration, notably:

- to promote the interconnection and interoperability of networks;
- to protect and enhance the trends towards the integration of advanced networks.

Such a desire not only applies to the physical infrastructure but also to all other parties and issues involved in network development. This includes equipment manufacturers, software developers, management of networks and tariffing of users. This integration concern is likely to be broadened as the liberalisation process proceeds.

The policy towards the telecommunications sector has evolved since 1984. Initially it focused upon the even development and application of ICTs and has since spread to the promotion of the information society. Policy has evolved from stressing relatively narrow themes to those that imply much broader socio-economic change. Much of the initial action was focused upon developing a coherent approach to establishing equipment and services. A coherent approach towards infrastructure came much later. EU policy on infrastructure has tended to focus upon using the central institutions as a forum for common network management and for co-ordinating network development within the member states.

Importantly for the purposes of infrastructure development, 1984 saw the launch of the scheme to oversee the co-ordinated introduction of ISDN[5] within the Community. The Action Plan[6] had six main themes:

- co-operation on ISDN;
- a fully integrated terminal market;
- co-operation in R&D;
- harmonious roll-out of telecommunications technology;
- consultation with industry on measures to be taken in telecommunications policy;
- common stance towards global communications.

These priorities shaped the form of policy as many follow-up measures stressed key issues of harmonisation, convergence and R&D. Thereafter this broad co-ordinative stance to network integration was complemented by the liberalisation process. The period prior to the initiation of EU-wide liberalisation focused upon what was seen as anticipated future development in telecommunications technology and networks. These were the first deliberate actions on the development of infrastructure.

Despite such action, policy did not seem to have much bite and infrastructure development remained relatively fragmented. Only some aspects of network development were being co-ordinated. This situation was not helped by ineffective standardisation measures. There was, in effect, no real momentum behind the desire to establish trans-European networks because the fragmentation of networks kept monopoly positions intact; a position few PTOs wanted to endanger.

Policy towards the development of infrastructure was only an implicit objective of the EU's assorted initiatives. Many schemes such as Esprit[7] were focused upon the IT sector. Their importance in terms of infrastructure only became apparent when technology drove the convergence of telecommunications and

40

IT, leading to a clearer perspective on the broader integration of the EU telecommunications sector. In practice, these early schemes had little supranational funding, but were useful frameworks for offering a co-ordinated approach to technological development. They did little for infrastructure as most states still introduced new networking technology along national standards (notably for ISDN).

Prior to the 1987 Green Paper,[8] Community action on telecommunications was focused upon ensuring co-ordination of R&D in areas of mutual interest. Interconnection and interoperability were frequently developed in basic forms of communication as a result of a series of bilateral/multilateral PTO agreements. Issues such as access and cohesion remained the concern of the respective member state. This scenario has changed due to technological developments, the rise of the network economy, the internationalisation of economies and the increased sophistication of users. Parochialism could no longer be justified in such an environment.

MARKET DEVELOPMENT OF NETWORKS

A major shift in the development of telecommunication networks came in the Green Paper of 1987. This sought to integrate and develop networks as a competitive response to market pressures. However, in practice these effects in terms of networks would not be felt equally across Europe. Broadly, this reregulation is in line with the market-led industrial policy of the EU, as commercial operators (both PTOs and non-PTOs) were expected to lead the process of network integration and development.

The Green Paper proposed the extension of SEM principles to this sector. Completion of this process is not expected until the beginning of the next millennium with the liberalisation of infrastructure. Such a policy expresses the resurgent belief in markets that has emerged in Europe over the last two decades. This position of faith, expressed by policy-makers and industry alike, is that if left largely to their own devices markets will develop the infrastructure to support the evolution of the information economy.

Extending the principles of the market to the development of telecom-TENs is a key strategy issue. The legacy of the market for the development of these networks, in terms of the TENs criteria, requires action (as reflected in Table 3.1) upon both the demand and supply sides of the telecommunications environment. Since not all of these actions are likely to be stimulated by the market and given that some are vital policy areas, measures to encourage their realisation are likely to be forthcoming. Consequently, policy is centred upon promoting the market-led diffusion of advanced communications and developing a set of measures that complements the commercial realisation of telecom-TENs. Ultimately policy must overcome any inertia within user and supplier communities that may impede network development (Stoneman 1987).

Table 3.1 Market for telecommunications and the TENs criteria

Market dimension	Network development policy
Network supply	Interconnection, interoperability, cohesion, access, standards, R&D
Network demand	Access, training, network dynamics

Despite evident problems, the process of liberalisation is perceived as pivotal in meeting, at least partially, key concerns of the development of telecom-TENs. More particularly, the promotion of integration and broader use of networks, via the application of markets, could feasibly enhance interconnection, interoperability and widen access. However, this still requires a series of complementary measures.

Initially liberalisation focused on the freeing up of the provision of value added services and equipment to complement the process of open network provision. The process within the EU is gradually shifting from service-based competition towards facilities-based competition.[9] The supranational policies have aimed to establish a minimum set of conditions for the development of a more commercially focused telecommunications environment within which advanced networks can emerge. This does not preclude some states from advancing further according to their preferences. Indeed, within the EU some states have already shifted towards facilities-based competition. Consequently, much of the supranational action is a consolidation of action already taken within some states. In this scenario, a key policy theme is to establish, via liberalisation, the conditions for the development of the network as a resource which can deliver increased value added from telecommunications to a broad range of users.

Service-based and facilities-based competition both have implications for the form and nature of the development of telecom-TENs, though each is likely to develop the system on a series of interconnected and interoperable networks. Under service-based competition, telecom-TENs have tended to emerge via a series of agreements between incumbent, frequently monopolistic, network operators. In this context, European networks are based upon a series of leased lines or inter-PTO agreements (see later). In the case of facilities-based competition, network ownership is more dispersed and there is a larger series of interconnection agreements. Where network ownership becomes more fragmented, standardisation issues become more pertinent for both users and suppliers. This is reflected in the increased diversity of membership of ETSI.

The impact of the existing service-based liberalisation upon telecom-TENs has been difficult to assess. While PTOs have increased investment in infrastructure, it is feasible that such expenditure could have been greater had they faced more intense competition. As a consequence many believe that in order to stimulate higher levels of investment in advanced infrastructure, facilities-based competition should be promoted (Stehmann 1995). The incentive for states to push for facilities-based competition frequently rests upon the experience of those who have advanced to this more mature form of liberalisation.

To date experience has shown that the move towards competition in infrastructure delivery is interlinked with the freer provision of telephony. There is evidence that if states want private investment then they have to enable suppliers to generate sufficient revenue streams to justify this outlay.[10] With voice telephony making up some 70 to 80 per cent of traffic, this will be a major incentive for new investors to provide the desired infrastructure.[11] However, many states are still reluctant to open up this core service to competition. Further incentives to liberalise rest upon a belief that the process will stimulate competitive benefits, via an improved networking environment, to the indigenous economy.[12]

Despite the initial and persistent reticence of many states towards the establishment of such a commercially led strategy, an evident consensus is emerging on the practicalities of this route for network investment. In the face of this broad consensus, many states are still reluctant fully to put this belief into practice, a fact reflected in the differing speed of implementation of the relevant legislation. Broadly, the more technologically advanced states are pushing ahead with liberalisation before the deadlines previously agreed while the cohesion states are generally lagging. In addition other states are reluctant to accept liberalisation due to the traditionally interventionist stance which they have taken towards network development.

It is important to ensure that shifts towards more diverse ownership, as engendered within facilities-based competition, do not endanger interoperability.[13] The nature of demand for telecommunications should ensure that new network owners have sufficient incentive to offer interoperability. ETSI standards are not mandatory but the nature of their evolution implies little encouragement to opt out of them. The development of voluntary standards as a means of achieving interoperability is promoted as a means to avoid the imposition of standards by a dominant state or the emergence of a *de facto* standard by a powerful economic group. Both of these scenarios could result in higher barriers to entry within the sector.

The importance of interoperability, within the development of telecom-TENs, underlines the significance of establishing the rules of interconnection for its constituent networks. The 'virtual' networking environment implies that interconnection will be via a series of multilateral agreements as opposed to the existing bilateral form. This interconnection issue is vital for it is estimated that it forms some 40 to 50 per cent of a new entrant's costs.[14]

The emergence of European networks is in response to the challenges imposed upon operators by the liberalisation process (see later). As a result telecom-TENs are developing as commercial rather than socio-economic phenomena. The short-term objective of liberalisation was to develop trans-national networks across the EU in reaction to commercial pressure. This sought to meet the immediate, though still very important, objective of enabling EU enterprises to derive greater value added from the network, a development that would be advantageous to the economy as a whole.

Despite such benefits, the ability of the network to meet broader concerns such as technological development and peripheral access would not generally be met over the short term. Such concerns need to be addressed if telecom-TENs are to be a true economic resource and complement the longer term objectives of harmonious economic development/regeneration and the establishment of the information society. This suggests a failure in the role of the EU to ensure that networks are managed to meet these priorities. It is important for the EU to develop a framework where the incentives exist, via liberalisation, for there to be a broader development of infrastructure to realise these objectives.

Many of the cohesion states[15] have opted for delays in the implementation of these directives in the fear that their relatively underdeveloped networks could suffer. This creates danger that they could be denied the investment needed in their infrastructure, thus increasing the technological divide. Clearly sparsely populated areas could suffer from a move to the market-based provision of infrastructure. Consequently some form of state investment in infrastructure needs to be maintained.

The slow response of some states to the process of liberalisation is based upon the premise that the best means of preserving access by all parts of the socio-economic strata is to deny access, at least initially, to other operators. These states are keen to preserve the integrity of the domestic telecommunications network at the possible danger of sustaining fragmentation. The split between states on liberalisation risks undermining the EU's credibility as a regulator. Thus the entire process of network management and progress towards telecom-TENs could be endangered. The development of telecom-TENs requires a convergence of network management techniques between states. If member states are going to do this then they are likely to require compensation from the centre to cover any problems of network access that could arise from such a strategy. Some advocate that a logical consequence of a convergence of network management rules is the creation of a single body to oversee the development of telecom-TENs.[16]

The cohesion issue aside, there have been other threats to the process. Freer competition on leased lines, a key component of liberalisation, has met with barriers. The main problem has been due to the fact that many operators have been slow to provide the information required to ensure that they are being treated fairly. Without this the anticipated gain in cheaper communications may be elusive. This undermines one of the fundamental objectives of the liberalisation process, namely the rebalancing of tariff structures by lowering the cost of international calls relative to local traffic. The knock-on effect is to limit the benefits derived to Europe from the development of the network economy.

This situation highlights how difficult the management of the liberalisation process has been and is likely to continue to be without some credible rule enforcer at supranational level. Lack of power on behalf of the Commission offers little incentive for some states to comply with directives.

The evolutionary path taken reflects the politics of the liberalisation process. The influx of competition, no matter at what pace, asks serious questions of the pre-competitive market structure. How incumbent operators respond can influence the speed towards a more liberal regime. Inevitably issues such as the legal status of *de facto* monopolies, the position of staff and volumes of employment will sway the politicians engaged in pushing the process forward. Greater efficiency is required if operators are to afford the level of network investment to sustain and maintain a position within a competitive telecommunications environment. Such domestic political problems can and have undermined the commitment by states to implement the liberalisation legislation.

The process of liberalisation within the EU has been slow. Only recently has a more concrete consensus on the role of markets gained credence among all states. Despite this the full liberalisation of the sector relies upon a continued commitment to the process by PTOs. While the EU has set dates and minimum forms of liberalisation, some states have proceeded faster than others. Generally the faster the state has proceeded towards liberalisation, the more advanced its telecommunications infrastructure has tended to be. The danger of some states lagging appears to be a restatement of the familiar theme of a multi-speed Europe, this time in technological development.

INTER-FIRM NETWORKS AND TENS

Chapter 2 highlighted the importance of inter- and intra-firm relationships in the development of the network economy. A feature of the process towards the realisation of telecom-TENs has been the rise of inter-firm networks as a means of developing the desired infrastructures. Such collaborations are increasingly central, alongside the liberalisation process, within the strategy for the evolving telecom-TENs. Generally these networks have been of two types:

- competitive networks: these take the form of strategic alliances to develop pan-European networks and to ensure the roll-out of advanced technology as a response to a competitive environment;
- pre-competitive networks: collaborations between actors to develop, interconnect and standardise emerging telecommunications technology before it is used in a competitive environment.

Chesnais (1988) noted that networks within the sectors are of specific types, as noted in Table 3.2.

The forms of alliances, that can occur within the sector, tend to establish both vertical and horizontal inter-relationships. In part, this can reflect the traditional interrelationships that existed before the trend towards reregulation took off. Evidently the rationale for each type of network will be different. With regard to industrial policy, it defines what role the EU sees in allowing collaboration

Table 3.2 Network relationships in telecommunications

Pre-competitive networks	Competitive networks	Competitive networks
Research and development	*Technological co-operation*	*Manufacturing and/or marketing co-operation*
• University based • Public/private co-operation • Research and development between corporations	• Small enterprises • Non-equity co-operation and research and development agreements • Technological agreements between enterprises	• Industrial joint ventures • Competitive R&D • Customer or supplier agreements • Licensing and marketing agreements

within an increasingly competitive environment. In the environment of a relatively passive industrial policy, the role of the public sector, either at national or supranational level, is based upon ensuring that such inter-relationships work to promote and not subvert the development of telecom-TENs.

COMPETITIVE NETWORK ALLIANCES AND TELECOM-TENS

These alliances[17] are often built around the desire to establish themselves as a European or global carrier for corporate communications. PTOs and other operators seek to establish an interconnected and interoperable network that offers a one-stop shop for corporate communications services. The objective is to develop this network to carry traffic that may have otherwise been delivered via a private network. In an era of globalisation and downsizing, the option of outsourcing corporate communications is attractive to many larger enterprises. The development of this market, and the accompanying alliances, is a direct result of the liberalisation process.

A prominent feature of the corporate communications environment is the delivery, in response to user demands, of global interoperability and the improved functionality of networks. Such user demands define telecom-TENs as a mere subnetwork of a holistic global infrastructure. The size of these large, increasingly global, carriers enables them to exploit bargaining power which can ensure leverage in price negotiation and greater economies of scale in network provision. Such benefits can be then passed on to the user in terms of improved communication services.

In this commercial context, trans-European telecommunication networks are largely based upon a series of Europe-wide backbones established by carrier alliances. These networks are based upon a series of interconnected nodes within specific states. The reach of the network is extended by the use of leased links and facilities. Such an extension is needed if these alliances are to deliver uniform functionality over their network. This places greater emphasis upon the interconnection, interoperability and, to some extent, access in the development of these networks. This is important for the TENs criteria will be reflected and in part necessitated by the commercial environment within which these networks are emerging. Despite developing their trans-European backbones, these alliances will still rely to some extent upon the incumbent operator to deliver the services to the door.

In this environment investment by these alliances in European infrastructure is occurring as a response to both endogenous (liberalisation) and exogenous influences (the demands of non-EU enterprises). This latter point is important. Given the trends to globalisation, foreign investors will consider the state of telecommunications infrastructure before investing in any area. In turn, European enterprises want good global connections to suppliers and markets overseas. These alliances reflect the growing global interdependence and eventual integration of what was a separate set of telecommunication networks. The fact that telecom-TENs are merely a piece of a larger global puzzle means that exogenous factors will contribute actively to the evolution of Europe's infrastructure. These factors underline the means by which such alliances could enhance competitive performance by the EU and its enterprises.

The advanced telecommunications infrastructure is developing as a result of user requirement for uniform Europe-wide functionality. The desire for each alliance to differentiate its services from others creates pressure for investment to ensure better transmission links and to update the nodes in these respective states to ensure harmonious functionality. Poor transmission links will limit the utility derived from the network and the competitiveness of the alliance. This user pressure is important. Not only does it influence infrastructure investment but also the R&D strategies of PTOs (see later).

These strategic alliances are designed to ensure market positioning, frequently by PTOs, within a competitive environment. Their development fits into the broad vision of how advanced networks are to be rolled out within the EU. As indicated in Figure 1.2, the EU strategy is based upon meeting the needs of enterprises which then spills over into the professions and the public domain.

Despite promoting aspects of the TENs criteria, these alliance-based, pan-European networks are not TENs in the sense that they are envisaged in the Maastricht Treaty. They do not seek to exhibit the broad social, economic and cultural objectives reflected within the policy priorities of the TENs initiative. However, this should not detract from their potential importance in the European networking environment. Clearly, in this instance, telecom-TENs are represented by the development of globally interoperable, common European backbones to deliver the functionality required to targeted niche user groups.

These alliance-based networks are likely to play an important function in the holistic development of TENs. To date their impact upon the EU's broad industrial policy objectives are limited. To ensure that they fulfil the requirements of the information society and complement networks being developed elsewhere is likely to depend upon a more fully ingrained information culture within European states and a more complementary regulatory structure. This highlights a priority for policy-makers. Despite such initial limitations in terms of telecom-TENs, these alliances are proving to be the motors of the roll-out of the technology tested in research networks that should further push the development and broader deployment of advanced networks. Some of these alliances are already planning the introduction of advanced networking into the public domain.[18]

There is no clear cut route as to how the establishment and evolution of these pan-European carrier networks will feed through into the holistic development of telecom-TENs. But within the context of the EU's market-based industrial policy they are important for their impact upon inter/intra-firm communications. These inter-firm networks reflect the practicalities of the environment within which PTOs find themselves. They allow firms to develop a uniform product over space based on a common infrastructure platform and technology and to create new interdependencies between equipment vendors,[19] telecommunication administrations and user groups.

Stehmann (1995) argues that the development of these alliances could have a negative effect upon the establishment of telecom-TENs. Their service-based approach to liberalisation, he argues, provides little incentive to invest in sufficient quantities to develop telecom-TENs.

Transnational alliances may seek to increase the quality of links between their nodes as a means of delivering, within agreed standards, a differentiated service and lower communication costs. However, the incentives to do so are lacking when liberalisation means that other alliances can benefit without investing themselves. Due to this free rider problem, a potential vicious circle in network investment results that could undermine the relative competitiveness of enterprises within this area.

As these alliances are market positioning devices, they deter other operators from entering the sector. Their market leverage, cost advantages and existing customer loyalty in the home markets could all represent prohibitive barriers to entry. If such a strategy is successful, any incentives for improved investment in infrastructures are further removed. As a result this co-operation, in developing Europe-wide networks, is based upon delivering trans-European services and not upon updating links or promoting the technological development of the economy.

Stehmann (1995) argues that the only way to break such a cycle is to shift to facilities-based competition so these PTO-based alliances have to invest as a response to entry, both actual and potential, within this sector. In the absence of facilities-based competition, PTOs have sought to improve the quality of leased line capacity via assorted pre-competitive agreement (see later).

A further concern for telecommunications is over the control of a bottleneck infrastructure and unfair practices in a sector with large entry barriers. While the former would be aided by facilities-based competition, the latter may decline as pressure upon PTOs increases from users as a result of liberalisation. It has already been shown with the EVPN[20] that anachronistic practices to limit competition in a global marketplace are not credible as users can shop elsewhere. Despite this, unfair practices are more significant when PTO revenues from the protected voice service monopolies can be used to subsidise value added series to undercut other service suppliers. This is an area where the EU's network management role has proved to be effective to some extent.[21]

A number of carriers has emerged to offer Europe-wide/global solutions to the increasing number of networked enterprises. Some such as SITA[21] were designed to support industry needs. Others such as Infonet were based almost solely upon alliances between a number of PTOs offering data solutions to business. In the light of the changing regulatory environment in Europe and beyond, there has been a number of emerging carriers based upon alliances between a number of PTOs such as Unisource, Global One and Concert. This has resulted in a series of competitive inter-firm networks that are operating against each other to capture an increased share of multinational communications.

Frequently these alliances are entities in their own right and their instability is a feature of the competitive and novel nature of the market. Some have already failed: notably Eunetcom,[23] Syncordia[24] and the SITA/Unisource link.[25] These failures show the risks involved in the market but also reflect the repositioning that goes on within these networks to strengthen competitive position.

Despite this the development of joint ventures only offers a partial solution to the development of TENs as clear dangers remain to interoperability, interconnection and universality. To avoid a scenario where telecom-TENs are not developed, there has to be a complementary set of policies to expand TENs along the lines envisaged within the criteria. These generally occur in the forum of pre-competitive relationships.

PRE-COMPETITIVE NETWORKS

These inter-firm networks reflect the increasingly complex interrelationships between companies within this sector. Most European PTOs are involved in such pre-competitive collaborations, reflecting the broad requirements and mutual interest in the development of advanced infrastructure. These networks are becoming increasingly diverse as the sector evolves technologically. Thus telecommunications operators become involved in network relationships with broadcasters, software and hardware developers and other manufacturers which have an interest in European network infrastructure evolution (see Figure 3.1).

Such collaborations aim to set the framework for the more fulsome development of networks under the competitive regime. In many cases, they may seek to introduce and test common standards or develop links to facilitate competition. Such pre-competitive interlinkages form the basis for the competitive roll-out of networks in an interconnected and interoperable fashion. This collaboration can either be industry-led, PTO-based or as a response to industrial policy pressure.

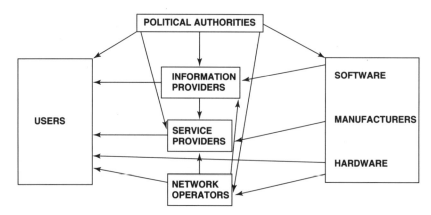

Figure 3.1 Emerging interrelationships in telecommunications
Source: Greenop, 1995

These co-ordinative agreements may have positive industrial impacts in enabling a more certain environment for investment and innovation and for the diffusion of new technology throughout an economic space.

Industry-led collaborations

Two notable collaborations are the technology forums that have been developed by PTOs (including EU and non-EU concerns) with equipment manufacturers. Notably there are industry-led forums for ATM,[26] Frame Relay[27] and two for VPNs.[28] All seek to advance network development and expand the value added derived from such technologies by introducing interoperability as an initial requirement. These forums are designed to promote the international integration of networks to meet, initially, the needs of MNCs. Thus the themes of global interconnection and interoperability are key issues and will inevitably have consequences for the roll-out of technology associated with telecom-TENs.

These forums are a formal expression of the degree of mutual interdependence that results from the common concerns of technology. Once the basic interoperability of these technologies is established then competitive roll-out occurs. Collaborations that deliver uniform functionality between services suppliers may only work to restrict technological development and will ultimately limit the intensity of competition within the sector. A collaboration that delivers such results works to no party's interests except perhaps to those who wish to re-monopolise the market.

These bodies reflect how modern communications standards need to be developed within an open environment. Over time the standards process has been splintered without any corresponding fragmentation within the sector. Ultimately the pace of technological change has driven these changes as the traditional standards bodies have taken longer to respond than industry.

European PTO-led collaborations

These collaborations are led by the dominant PTOs in Europe, often within the scope of ETSI, to ensure basic interoperability and interconnection of advanced networks. The importance of ETSI as a forum should not be underestimated in the development of TENs; it is a practical expression of the concern of all bodies in network evolution. Such collaborations include the General European Network (GEN) and the Managed European Transmission Network (METRAN).

Such initiatives, which involve direct improvement in the quality of the infrastructure on a pan-European basis, are a direct response to the liberalisation process. While they are not linked to the telecom-TENs programme, they are likely to prove important for the overall development of the European telecommunications environment, especially infrastructure. In the short term, they are focused on a narrow market niche but their use is likely to be broadened to more aspects of the socio-economic strata as the information society is established.

Such collaborations have been supplemented by a number of Memorandums of Understanding (MoUs) between major PTOs upon evolving technology. These seek to introduce a co-ordinated approach to the introduction of the successor networks that are the basis of the evolution of telecom-TENs. Thus far, MoUs have been signed upon the introduction of E-ISDN and ATM. They are experiments to test new technology and services and seek to ensure that the service offered, notably in the case of E-ISDN, is of a minimum standard. In the case of the ATM MoU, the members have established a collaborative network as a means of testing this new technology.[29]

The interlinkages have been further strengthened by a new collaborative R&D institute, EURESCOM.[30] This is an offshoot of the CEPT[31] involving 23 PTOs from 18 European states. The aims of EURESCOM are to ensure interoperability of services and to promote the dissemination of R&D throughout the EU. This body is a clear link to the fulsome development of telecom-TENs and provides interlinkages between competitive and pre-competitive alliances. It also aims to complement the introduction of global standards, stimulate and co-ordinate field trials, and harmonise national strategies while not inhibiting competition between the companies concerned. The body is not authoritative since there are no obligations on behalf of the states to obey its recommendations.

EURESCOM's role within the competitive environment is to ensure that the basic building blocks of advanced European networking are developed; notably with regard to a reliable pan-European infrastructure. These pre-competitive building blocks are of mutual concern and reflect a desire for PTOs to work together to establish the infrastructure, as well as the interfaces, procedures and protocols for services. In practical terms, for the development of telecom-TENs, EURESCOM has undertaken work upon intelligent networks and sought to harmonise strategies, carried out trials for METRAN and performed tests for the ATM network.

In many ways the establishment of relationships such as those for EURE-SCOM is symptomatic of the competitive environment within which PTOs now operate. The collaboration at pre-competitive stages represents an avenue for economies. Many of these joint ventures, though designed independently of the TENs initiative, are in some aspects pushing their development along commercial lines. The requirements of a standardised format for the delivery of commercially based services is proving to be the main driver behind such developments.

The need to develop standards to work for the mutual interest of companies has been a powerful force in the promotion of collaboration. As the development of a network occurs alongside the liberalisation of other aspects of the telecommunications sector, so there is a greater diversity of interest in the manner in which these networks develop. Notably the development of advanced networks involves inter-relationships between PTOs, satellite companies, LAN companies, etc.[32] Technological advancement, especially when it involves liberalisation, is an increasingly pluralistic affair. These forms of collaboration provide an opportunity for reducing uncertainty and exploiting synergies among operators.

Not all joint ventures have been successful. For example, in the 1980s European PTOs collaborated upon the Managed Data Network Services project; another failure was the EBIT (European Broadband Interconnection Trial) programme whose poor performance led the EU to withdraw support (see later).

ETSI AND THE EII

ETSI was a direct result of the requirements of the 1987 Green Paper and its development is central to the evolution of TENs as it seeks to ensure interoperability and interconnection of these infrastructures. The body brings together all interested parties including manufacturers, PTOs and users. Essentially it is a public–private partnership that sets the framework for the development of European telecommunications. Its industrial policy consequences stem from the desirable cost effects bred from the more rational use and advancement of Europe's networks. These benefits can fall to PTOs, equipment manufacturers and, perhaps more importantly, users. Its action is to complement the liberalisation process in order to ensure that it works to the mutual advantage of all participants within the European theatre. ETSI collaborates with other standards bodies to ensure an holistic approach to the development of the EU's IT sector. A result of this work, and the increased utilisation of both ISDN and broadband technology, is the proposed European Information Infrastructure (EII): an initiative further championed by the European Commission.

The EII is the contribution of ETSI towards the development of telecom-TENs. Its role within telecom-TENs is to complement and plot the holistic development of the ISDN and IBC in the EU. The EII should seek to evolve with the networking environment and is more of a concept than a new network. The initiative is initially based upon the desire to act upon programmes taken within Japan and the USA to develop advanced infrastructure. The aim is to take the lead to ensure that European standards become the global norm. Such a stance has inevitable industrial policy implications by potentially enabling the IT sector first-starter advantages in this area. To ensure this scenario is realised, ETSI is collaborating with the ITU[33] to ensure the interoperability of the EII with other networks. While the main development and deployment of these networks is in the domain of operators, ETSI will carry out the major standardisation work. The EII is concerned with standardising networks in an environment where network ownership is likely to become more diverse. The concern of ETSI is that such developments should not impede interoperability, universality and interconnection. It is in the commercial interests of all that future networks do not develop along the lines of their predecessors, and that integration happens from day one and not as an afterthought.

The EII, like telecom-TENs, is a federation of separate networks. The essential aim is to provide a common stance on network development, thereby preventing new barriers to the integration of European telecommunications. This is represented by a policy stance that takes a holistic view of the increasingly dispersed network development and deployment. The EII is not a stationary concept but designed to evolve with technology. Thus in the initial phases it will stress ISDN with a planned evolution into broadband, a transformation envisaged as market-led.

In the development of these networks, the parties involved cover all areas of the globe. Those involved worked to ensure that the EII developed in a manner that was agreed to common objectives and standards. In many ways such a stance is too late for ISDN but is based upon ensuring that successor networks, notably TEN-IBC, advance according to mutual requirements.

Two phases are planned for the EII, underlining its evolutionary nature:

- First Generation EII: involving the consolidation of existing technologies such as N-ISDN, PSTN and early broadband into an effective single network. This may imply some reorientation of existing networks.
- Second Generation EII: involving the harmonised introduction of ATM and other forms of broadband technologies.

There are inevitably parallels between the industry-led EII and the development of telecom-TENs. While both are concerned to ensure interoperability and interconnection and complement the universality concerns associated with liberalisation, differences do exist. As a policy measure telecom-TENs are, in part, designed to promote the broad concerns of socio-economic cohesion and development. The EII has clearer commercial overtones and is focused upon standardisation for this reason. Despite such differences, both have the common concern of using advanced networks to deliver competitive benefit to European-based enterprises. The broader policy concerns of the telecom-TENs initiative differentiates the two. There can be no doubt that the EII will contribute to the development of TENs by setting the standards under which the commercial concerns will develop networks. An additional important factor will be the promotion of the external connection of telecom-TENs. In part, the EII is a result of the commercial strategy followed by the EU and its desire to get the private sector involved in the advancement of infrastructure. Given such developments, the EU is likely to wish to ensure that they do not work to the detriment of the wider concerns involved in TENs. The EU is therefore required to take a pro-active role in the network management.

Industrial policy-induced collaborations

One of the more pro-active forms of collaboration has been those encouraged, as part of a wider policy process, to support the common development of ICTs. Much of the action at the supranational level is designed to support alliances between firms to develop ICTs of common interest. The various schemes have a large number of interlinkages, with many enterprises being part of different pre-competitive networks. In the specific plans for telecommunications networks, the EU has sought to promote advanced communications for SMEs and to facilitate the ability of enterprises to pursue broadband communications. These industrial policy initiatives (which are currently part of the Fourth Framework Programme) reflect the common concerns of technology and aim to contribute to the market-led attainment of telecom-TENs (see Table 3.3). They also seek to attain the global interoperability and interconnection of telecom-TENs. In planning terms, this reflects the need to see telecom-TENs as a mere sub-network of a larger whole. Consequently one of the EU's network management functions is to create international alliances in the development of telecom-TENs.

The schemes being promoted at supranational level are designed to complement the development of telecom-TENs. This stance reflects some degree of political compromise in the promotion and funding of such schemes. Their interlinkages are important to underline as ACTS (software, micro-processing and multi-media) are to be integrated via Esprit in hard systems and applications. The telematics programme will seek to use this technology to focus on the application of these developments to specific areas of the economy. Building on previous initiatives, these schemes ultimately seek to ensure the spread of these technologies as broadly as possible throughout the socio-economic strata. The aim is to manage them to enable the telecommunications network to become a true asset to all forms and sizes of enterprise.

The EU's research policy has received criticism from certain parties.[34] The main problem concerns the fact that its focus upon pre-competitiveness limits the effects on the international standing of the European ICT sector. The policies place little emphasis upon the need to exploit the research findings. Technologies are targeted without sufficient understanding of how they are to be exploited to strengthen the commercial positioning of this sector. The Commission likes to separate its research actions from those dedicated to market-driven activities and is unwilling to combine the two.

Table 3.3 Industrial policy initiatives and TENs

Scheme	Link to requirement of TENs	Indicative network relationships
Esprit	• Support wide access to IT across a broad range of groups • Promote dissemination of best method • Compatibility of IT	Industry, users, universities, research centres
ACTS	• Advanced communication systems to aid economic development and cohesion • Promote access to advanced networks • Interconnection and interoperability of advanced networks	Network operators, equipment manufacturers, service vendors, end users and the possibility of SMEs International collaboration (Japan, USA)
Telematics	• Assist rural areas • Interconnection and interoperability • Promote broad application of this technology	Users, universities, IT companies, communication companies

R&D has often been seen as distant from the needs of the average European. This attitude has changed as successive programmes have grown closer to the end user. This trend has been promoted by the process of liberalisation and the Single Market.

NETWORK MANAGEMENT: THE EU'S PASSIVE ROLE IN TELECOM-TENS

The EU's dual role in network development is reflected in its desire to:

• avoid dominance of the European telecommunications market by foreign companies;
• gain a foothold in major markets;
• promote a common stance to the world;
• develop network as a true resource for all;
• develop EC factor productivity.

If TENs are to work according to the criteria laid out within the Treaty upon European Union, and fully complement the EU's industrial policy, then market-based actions facilitated by liberalisation need to be supplemented. A network management role by the EU implies involvement in both the development of telecommunication networks and the inter-firm networks inherent in their realisation. These revolve around a series of rules, regulations and actions that encourage the private sector, in combination with the public sector where required, to develop telecom-TENs in the desired manner.

The ambition of such a role is to encourage the market to develop tele-communication networks in a manner that meets the EU's industrial policy objectives. Much of the dilemma within network management stems from the perceived competition/co-operation trade-off that is believed to be endemic within this sector. Too much competition is seen as a risk inducer and a barrier to European technological advancement, whereas collaboration may lead to a re-monopolisation of the market. It is apparent that neither extreme of competition or collaboration will enable telecom-TENs to be fully realised. The EU and the other regulatory bodies are therefore in a policy scenario where these twin concerns need to be balanced as a means of meeting telecom-TENs. There are two basic prongs in the EU's process towards network management:

- ensuring, via liberalisation, that markets are free to deliver the finance needed for TENs;
- ensuring that any market failures which emerge from the liberalisation process are counteracted so that they do not endanger the holistic completion and attainment of TENs.

Much of the focus of this chapter has centred on the idea of what is required of telecommunication networks in order to fulfil the TENs criteria. In the case of liberalisation, policy is designed to promote harmonious network management standards to ensure that access concerns are met. ONP is primarily about access to the network in non-discriminatory terms. Broad and total access will only be fully achieved when a pluralist set of networks allows all parties that wish to access it the right to do so. The EU has also welcomed within certain limits the emerging alliances and other forms of collaboration. It sees these as an integral part of its strategy to realise telecom-TENs and its network management role defines the framework under which these agreements can emerge.

The development of a network management role involves treatment of the network as a common asset which is governed by a common set of rules and pro-tocols. The management of the network has to ensure that sufficient potential revenue is generated to encourage entry into the sector and increase investment in network infrastructure. This is necessary to provide sufficient incentives to stimulate the commercial investment of the network as required by the EU's industrial strategy. If the existence of such incentives prohibit the development of the network as a true economic resource to all layers of the socio-economic strata, then liberalisation will need to be complemented by a series of public sector actions. Consequently the major network management roles that will be the focus of this area of industrial policy are:

- co-ordination of national policies;
- promotion of competition;
- developing standards;
- developing and implementing financing mechanisms;
- promoting technological cohesion;

- establishing global interfaces;
- education of users, providers and suppliers and creating demand.

In combination, these measures will enable the EU to generate the critical mass to sustain the private-led development of networks in the desired manner. By promoting the demand for these technologies, together with the exploitation of network externalities, this policy should deliver universal interconnection and interoperability as well as enhancing roll-out.

Policy has to be holistic in its approach, appreciating the interlinkages between all areas of telecommunications in the evolution of TENs. The EU will not develop its management role in isolation since its policy initiatives are set within a broad framework which includes working within the broad remit of the subsidiarity principle, working with the assorted standardisation bodies (CEN,[35] CENELEC,[36] ETSI), co-operating with industry and user bodies (such as ECTUA[37] and ETNO[38]) and establishing interoperability with other networks.

Competition, liberalisation and TENs

Since the 1987 Green Paper, liberalisation has been complementary to the strategy for market-led TENs. It has provided opportunities for EU firms to establish a global presence in certain areas of the market while creating a framework for harmonious network development. The recognition of the global economic importance of telecommunications is pushing many states to advance the liberalisation of the sector before the deadlines set.[39] This requires co-ordination between states that often have different perspectives on the role of telecommunication networks. Consequently the EU needs to be a credible regulator to ensure compliance. To assist in this, an overarching regulatory commission has been mooted. Traditionally the EU relies upon commercial and competitive pressure to force states to meet the requirements. In some cases this has proved effective, in others less so.[40] Another concern has been that competition should not self-destruct. There has to be some attempt by the EU to manage the inter-firm networks to ensure the market-led strategy is not endangered.[41]

It has already been seen that the inter-firm networks are proving to be a fairly effective device for infrastructure investment. There are expectations that this investment will increase further when full liberalisation has occurred within the EU. Yet these agreements, whether at the pre-competitive or competitive stage, need a framework within which to operate. ONP has defined the access rights. It is up to the EU to establish the relationship between the developing inter-firm networks and competition law.

The EU has published guidelines which reflect the balancing act it has to perform in ensuring that technological progress is not hindered by over-zealous competition law.[42] The EU will allow and even encourage agreements that foster interconnection, interoperability and technological development insofar as such agreements do not seek to limit effective competition. There will inevitably be agreements that restrict competition, but these are only granted with strict guarantees – notably Global One and Unisource/Telefonica. These alliances were only granted regulatory approval if all participants advanced the liberalisation process within their indigenous markets. It is important that the EU's network management role should be seen as a device to deter practices that will inhibit the private and holistic development of telecom-TENs.

Universal service obligations and peripheral access

The ultimate aim of the information society is for all people to have access to the technology and services associated with these changes. Hence many of the applications favoured by the EU are concerned with encouraging access to advanced networks by SMEs, schools, hospitals and other public services. This strategy seeks to create 'an information culture' and prevent the emergence of information haves and have nots. This needs to be complemented by policies that stimulate the demand for ICTs by training initiatives. Access requires flexibility in the face of changing technologies, connectivity and equity (Hudson 1994); to promote access fully these need to be complemented by affordability.

Broad access is a necessary prerequisite to the information society. The lucrative business market, which is attracting most investment, only represents some 25 to 30 per cent of all users. The ability of commercial operators to supply the rest depends upon the relevance of advanced services to this segment of the market. Such demand is still uncertain and this situation is likely to persist until a holistic information culture is present.

Infrastructure within the EU needs to develop in a manner that does not deliberately deny access to any area or social group. As part of the development of telecom-TENs this implies:

- a definition of universal service;
- renewal of the local loop;[43]
- state-assisted investment in those locations where market failure may occur.

The notion of universal service obligation has four basic aspects (Cave *et al.* 1994):

- geographical coverage;
- geographical averaging of tariffs;
- low access charges for residents;
- targeted subsidies.

The strategy to achieve TENs leaves open to debate the notion of access. Inevitably suppliers are going to be concerned with effective demand and not need. Consequently the EU has pushed for Universal Services Objectives (USO) to be defined as part of the liberalisation process. The whole concept is shrouded in ambiguity, only committing suppliers to a reasonable level of service. The funding of USO is also for debate and a number of different schemes has been proposed such as contributions towards a central USO fund. When defining minimum service it is important to understand that the notion of USO is a variable concept which will alter as users become more sophisticated and technology more affordable.[44] Preserving access and ensuring that the information society has its desired effects means that advanced infrastructure has to reach all households via the local loop. Such a process is inevitably costly and will take place on an evolutionary basis.

The need for wholesale replacement of fibre for copper in the local loop is an obvious barrier. In the EU, three trends are emerging to push for the development of the local loop (Analysys 1995):

- cable television is relaying the local access network;
- compression technologies;
- radio in the local loop.

Such trends are inevitably linked into the continued commercialisation of networks as an immediate facilitator of this investment. Generally this process has developed fastest where regulatory restrictions have been lightest. Therefore the regulatory structure is important in determining the conditions of access and the rights of all users to utilise all services. The role of the state is to avoid what Hudson (1994) calls 'electronic balkanisation'. This is required for the full absorption of states into a unified system.

The other major concern is in ensuring the equality of access across space. Thus under the structural funds the EU has developed schemes such as STAR[45] and Télématique to offer advanced communications to peripheral areas.[46] This underlines the potential that the EU believes telecommunications to have in promoting regional development (Capello 1994). A lower level of potential users, and therefore lower network externalities and less impetus toward attaining a critical mass, means that network development in these areas requires an active push. The growth of infrastructure within these parts makes information more widely available than before. Much of the EU telecommunications effort on network development has been traditionally focused in peripheral areas .[47]

Existing experience has highlighted that liberalisation does little to reduce disparities in telecommunications. In the core areas choice of operators has tended to increase markedly whereas in the periphery a monopoly frequently remains.[48] Despite policy initiatives, it is unlikely that peripheral areas will exhibit the same degree of technological sophistication as core regions. Universal service obligation has an evident territorial dimension that takes on a new perspective under liberalisation. These issues are addressed to ensure that the expected benefits of the shift to the information society are felt throughout Europe's economic space. The regional aspect of the development of the information society is also important in that it provides a useful laboratory to analyse its effects.

Global interoperability and interconnection

There are a number of differing EU initiatives to be taken into account when developing telecom-TENs. One factor is the collaboration with the other G7 members to develop a common framework for these infrastructures. In very broad terms, these G7 concerns echo those inherent within telecom-TENs and the strategy to achieve them. The only difference is that issues such as interoperability and interconnection and access now apply globally. The G7 has agreed to undertake joint research upon a number of key areas. Such initiatives are born out of the mutual interest among all G7 states to ensure that they stay ahead of the field in these areas. Of importance within these projects are those that seek to ensure global interoperability of broadband networks and to address issues of common concern such as awareness of ICTs and training in their usage. The aim is to create a global network of networks. This G7 initiative supports President Clinton's proposal for a Global Information Infrastructure (GII) with global interoperability and interconnection governed by a common, harmonised set of conventions.

The EU is not the only body concerned with the development of global networks as the ETSI initiative, EII, is set within the broad context of the GII. The EII is designed to complement and be interoperable with the NII (National Infrastructure Initiative) and the High Performance Info-Communications Infrastructure in Japan. These schemes are all of a similar model though the systems and strategy for their development do differ.[49] It is within this broad context that telecom-TENs need to be examined and their development managed. Such a strategy of mutuality in infrastructure development recognises the spillovers and externalities inherent in infrastructure within an emerging global network economy.

Financing

The EU hopes that the vast majority of funding for telecom-TENs comes from commercial operators. Despite this, the Commission plans to supplement this with its own resources to ensure that the networks develop in line with its broad industrial policy objectives. Inevitably much of the financial support for TENs would come through PPPs, indirectly through initiatives to promote the information society or via direct supranational support. The TENs budget line enables the EU to utilise those resources that it does possess to develop infrastructure along the lines envisaged within the Maastricht Treaty. These are funds designed to enhance access to ICTs and promote network development in peripheral areas. Within the telecommunications sector much of this is going to be focused upon the basic networks and a forum within which basic applications and services can be tested and eventually deployed. Given that the cost of these networks is some ECU150,[50] billion over the five years up to 2000 the TENs budget, and any monies available for network development in peripheral areas, can only contribute small amounts to the development of telecommunication networks.

Determining use of networks and deployment

The development of these networks as a complement to industrial policy is reflected in the strategy chosen; a market route with limited direction from the public sector. The Commission has been keen to have some say in the development of the uses of networks to ensure that value added and access are maximised. In terms of assistance, it has tended to focus upon social, cultural and economic applications and not the potential mass market applications such as teleshopping and video-on-demand. This is based upon the desire to develop a culture that accepts information as a social and economic necessity and not purely as a form of entertainment. In the USA, strategy has focused upon these mass applications, though in practice business demand is still driving roll-out. The EU aims to develop more business-based services first and then shift to the mass market. Much of the EU financing is focused upon demonstrating that these applications are profitable to the private sector.

A further aspect is the measures taken by the EU to push the deployment of the technology associated with TENs. To aid this, it has established a multi-annual telecom-TENs initiative. The programme aims to support projects utilising existing technology that promote the broader use and marketability of telecom-TENs as a means of attaining the critical mass needed to sustain the commercial roll-out of the network.

Network management and industrial policy

From the above, it should be evident that the development of telecommunication networks requires some sort of public sector action to ensure that the strategy for their development is not compromised and that market failures do not deter their full realisation. The endpoint of such actions is to enable all parts of Europe to access advanced communications at a reasonable price. Such developments will seek to benefit enterprises not only by delivering lower communication costs but also by aiding the establishment of a labour force that utilises information in a manner that is to the benefit of the economy. According to the Commission's viewpoint, the development of ICTs should also aid the cohesion aspect of policy. In an environment where space is becoming less of an issue, the development of telecommunication networks offers opportunities to enhance economic development of peripheral areas.

Table 3.4 reflects the interaction of network management, TENs and industrial policy. The development of telecommunications as a true resource

Table 3.4 Network management and industrial policy

Network concern	Action
Universality: access	Co-ordination on universal service objectives, telematic programmes of common interest, training schemes for ICTs, application of ONP
Universality: cohesion	Regional development initiatives from structural funds, European Investment Bank, European Investment Fund, co-ordinate national initiatives, rural telematics initiatives
Interconnection	Standardisation, industry forums, competition policy, research framework, managing competitive alliances
Interoperability	Standardisation bodies, internal collaboration, co-ordination of national networks, competitive alliances

and the establishment of a level of demand for these services to justify telecom-TENs has to be based ultimately upon a broad realisation of how important are advanced telecommunications for economic development and regeneration. Only when there is evident demand for services will the development of the network take on its own momentum free from state assistance. This underlines the importance of awareness and training schemes in the broad population. The greater the familiarity with ICTs, the more labour skills should reflect changing labour demand. These in turn should stimulate a supply-side response in terms of factors such as economies of scale. The combination of these factors is pivotal in stimulating the market for telecom-TENs.

The Commission has taken active measures, as part of the European Social Fund, to improve the training schemes linked to the process of structural change. Partnerships have also been fostered to ensure that the challenges imposed upon the labour market by structural change are met. These measures largely complement those taken at the national level and the deployment strategies noted above.

CONCLUSION

The key problem stems from the difference between telecom-TENs as a public policy measure and telecom-TENs as a commercial phenomena. The liberalisation route towards TENs only provides a partial answer for their development. While it may generate flows of investment, the requirements of TENs as an integral part of Europe's Competitiveness Strategy requires public bodies to perform a network management role. The basis of such action is to ensure that all requirements of TENs are met via a series of complementary public and private sector actions. The basis of these complementary actions in the development of TENs is designed to address issues of market failure. The TENs criteria require that such action is needed. If these networks are to support the development of the information society they must be ubiquitous in coverage.

The development of criteria within the TENs initiative will not only affect the market-led strategy but also be affected by it. If states push for universality, in terms of coverage and access, this may create a critical mass to allow the full development of TENs to occur. States therefore need to put into place inter-operable networks and encourage the development of this technology in areas where the market would not do so.

4

THE INTEGRATED SERVICES DIGITAL NETWORK AS A TRANS-EUROPEAN NETWORK (TEN-ISDN)

INTRODUCTION

The previous chapter outlined the belief that if the EU is to develop telecom-TENs in the desired fashion then it has to take on some form of network management role. The aim of this chapter is to see how far the EU has to perform this role with regard to the commercial development of the Integrated Services Digital Network as a trans-European network (TEN-ISDN). While ISDN is an intermediate network, its importance to the information society is in the delivery of advanced services and applications over existing infrastructure.[1] ISDN is perceived as an important initiator for a sustained promotion of the information society. As such the network and the associated services/applications provided should assist in the smooth migration to successor networks.

It is important to underline that the EU has for some time given implicit support to the development of ISDN via stimulating moves towards the establishment and adoption of commonly agreed standards (E-ISDN). This is perceived as a necessary precursor to the more holistic development of TEN-ISDN. More recently the EU has grown active in measures to seek its deployment. The basis of the strategy to achieve TEN-ISDN is to utilise and manage market forces to ensure that national ISDN evolves into an effective interoperable and interconnected network of networks. The aim is to use the network as a common resource for the development of services and applications that complement the EU's broad industrial policy objectives.

This chapter seeks to examine how the public and private sectors interact to develop a strategy to establish ISDN as a TEN. Initially this chapter explores the nature of ISDN and how it has evolved under national guidance in an incompatible and fragmented manner. The problems experienced by the market for the technology in attaining a critical mass are also examined. Schemes utilising E-ISDN are explored as a means of delivering a network of networks which is the basis of TEN-ISDN, together with the EU's network management function in the attainment of this objective.

DEVELOPMENT OF ISDN IN EUROPE

Within the context of the EU's telecommunications policy, ISDN is seen as a stepping-stone between the analogue infrastructure and its evolution into an integrated broadband network. ISDN provides the delivery channels for advanced services and is therefore not a service in its own right. Its importance lies in the fact that the digitalisation of the network allowed services to be integrated and therefore offered over single rather than multiple networks. Such a feature facilitated the potential for the increased exploitation of economies of scale and scope in network deployment and development. This could prove pivotal in the technological advancement of the economy. The importance of ISDN is enhanced by the fact that it utilises existing copper-based infrastructure to deliver digital services. This means that greater functionality can be derived from existing infrastructure without requiring, over the short term at least, a large-scale relaying of the network.

ISDN is in part a response of the PTOs to the merging of the separate telecommunications and computing environments and the impact this has had or is likely to have upon traffic (Noam 1990). As a technology, ISDN has been in existence since the late 1970s, but has only been pushed commercially with any great zeal since the mid-1980s. The functionality of the network in the EU is generally limited to 2 Mbp/s, though this may be augmented by the increased application of data compression technologies.[2]

The development of ISDN is being driven by the demand for high-speed data communications, something for which the analogue technology is unsuited. In many sectors of the network economy, data are superseding voice transmission as the primary utilisation of telecommunications. This is especially true for business communications. The digitalisation of the network is deemed to offer advantages to enterprises in terms of speed, quality, flexibility and international dimension. This is vital to the understanding of the technology, the manner of its commercial development and its impact upon economic performance.

The switch to an ISDN is justified in terms of rationalising the amount of Customer Premises Equipment (CPE) associated with ever more advanced networking. The roll-out of ISDN has been retarded by a lack of incentive to invest in this technology because many of the applications that it currently delivers can already be performed by existing technology, even though via different access points and equipment. Its commercial roll-out depends upon it delivering innovative services and increased value added to enterprises and proving that it is a generic and not a specialist technology.

In terms of the EU's industrial strategy, the importance of ISDN lies in the perceived economic advantages with all users being able to access some form of advanced network (see later). Any activism in this domain, limited though it may be, is designed to create scope for widespread deployment of ISDN. This action supports a need created by the development of the Single European Market (SEM) notably in terms of data communications. The SEM has tended to focus attention upon developing applications and generic services that, though available nationally, are able to support the anticipated increased interactions across borders that have resulted from these legislative changes.

ISDN is expected to become the predominant network infrastructure in Europe in the 1990s and to provide the initial means of supporting the objectives of the evolving information society. In practice, ISDN is likely to prove a transitory technology that will be superseded by a general shift to broadband in the formative years of the next millennium. Consequently, ISDN's importance for industrial policy also rests upon the expectation that it will provide a testbed for more advanced networking. Once the network is deployed more fully and its services/applications consumed more readily then the technology can be utilised to meet the challenges posed by the rise of the information society. The Commission hopes the European suppliers of ISDN are able to exploit the development of this indigenous market to strengthen their global position.

The development of ISDN in the EU has occurred via a series of nationally defined ISDN islands. The development of TEN-ISDN is not simply about interconnecting them but taking a holistic perspective of their evolution. Network development requires common standards, interconnecting national networks and ensuring that no part of the EU is denied access to this technology. The rise of the network economy is breeding an interdependence between national networks that is creating commercial pressure for integration. As such, national networks are evolving to stress the common standard: E-ISDN (see below).

Where it was offered as a commercial service, ISDN was based upon national models of the technology. These differ in terms of services supported and the way they are encoded and transferred by common protocols. This created difficulties in terms of international interworking of CPE and increased the expense of deployment and development of the network. Much debate continues as to whether ISDN is in fact a useful technology for Europe's economy or if it is just an irrelevant, outmoded stage in the evolution of telecommunication networks.[3]

British Telecom was the first European PTO to offer ISDN commercially, though it focused much of its efforts upon providing an international service, in preference to a domestic one. Via a series of bilateral agreements, BT developed a strong external dimension for both its primary (ISDN-30) and basic (ISDN-2) services.[4] The strong external focus of BT's service has made it generally much more flexible in response to the development of common international standards. Indeed both BT services are now compatible with ETSI's I.421 protocol.[5] This reflects the commerciality of the service and the relative maturity of the UK's telecommunications market which, in turn, reflects the liberal leanings of the regulatory regime.

France has strongly promoted ISDN as a public access network and has invested heavily to develop innovative applications relevant to this concern. As FT has developed the technology as a universal network it has sought to introduce it in a manner that is compatible with the themes of its industrial policy. Breeding a familiarity with the possibilities of ISDN is a key factor in the strategy of FT. Consequently FT has established partnerships with industry to achieve this objective. The ISDN market is focused upon business applications, though there has been a gradual encroachment into residential and SME markets. The high digitalisation of the FT network has assisted its relatively fulsome development. The French ISDN service, Numeris, reached national coverage in the early 1990s and its internationalisation has proceeded via a series of bilateral agreements. It has taken a gradual approach to the introduction of E-ISDN compatible services.

Germany has pushed ISDN as a stepping stone to broadband technologies. To this end it has sought to promote demand as a means of justifying a widespread shift to the more advanced networking technologies. It has offered favourable terms for ISDN use. Traditionally roll-out was impeded by poor digitalisation of the German network and lack of commitment to ISDN as a technology in its own right. ISDN has therefore been slow to take off within Germany, a fact compounded by low user interest (Arlandis 1994). Take-up of ISDN has been assisted by a greater degree of commitment to the technology by DT. Using the French model of partnerships, it has sought to develop more innovative applications. The fact that broadband is still someway off has bred a need for an intermediate technology to meet the demands of business. This has pushed the roll-out of ISDN in Germany over the last few years.

Under the development of ISDN by national PTOs, the establishment of interconnection and interoperability, albeit in a limited form, has occurred via a series of bilateral agreements. These have largely been self-serving and based upon meeting the requirements of indigenous enterprises. They have also sought to ensure the marketing of PTOs' services within a rival market. Such agreements have tended to limit the functionality derived from the network and they are gradually being replaced by the E-ISDN standard (see below) as ISDN in Europe develops within a multilateral forum, ETSI.

Where ISDN did not develop over the public network it grew on a private basis. Private suppliers such as Siemens and Bosch sought to meet the needs of private clients. Frequently this led to incompatibilities between the networks of rival private suppliers. As ISDN developed at different rates there was no evident need for standardisation. When the demand for ISDN increased the need for standardisation became more evident. Over time ETSI has sought to ensure that both public and private forms of ISDN are interoperable.

Overall the development of the ISDN in Europe has exhibited incompatibility and fragmentation, with limited harmonious functionality and uneven development of services and applications. Many of the incompatibilities were due to differences in the implementation of ISDN equipment where differing specifications meant that CPE often lacked interoperability. This hampered the potential of the market by increasing the cost of CPE and reducing the functionality of the network (Public Network Europe 1995b).

The bilateral agreements for interconnection and interoperability were not holistic in developing a network of networks. Consequently TEN-ISDN remained elusive. This position was compounded by the lack of any specific commitment to its attainment by network operators. This was partly due to substantive differences between member states on the role of networks which led to divergence in approaches. Some states have been keen to push broad access to the technology whereas others have been much more market driven. As a result ISDN has not developed as a TEN but as a series of networks that have been integrated on an *ad hoc* basis as the nature of business communications has altered.

The development of ISDN as a pan-European resource is initially to be focused on meeting the requirements of commercial operators. Much of the strategy to develop ISDN as a TEN is based upon managing and utilising market forces to deliver this technology across a broad range of socio-economic groups and regions. This initially means supporting the commercial exploitation of the technology and utilising this critical mass to support its broader development.

MARKET DRIVERS OF ISDN

At the heart of the Commissions strategy for ISDN is 'to develop the conditions for the market to provide European Users with a greater variety of telecommunication services'.[6] Consequently, TEN-ISDN relies upon utilising commercial forces for its deployment as a support for the rise of the information society. Yet despite being commercially available for over a decade in Europe, ISDN has been slow to exhibit any sustained signs of roll-out into the public network. There are many reasons for this but much rests upon the uncertainty associated with this technology and its perceived failure to deliver anything that was either different from existing network offerings or really needed.[7]

In practice, ISDN developed as a technology before any practical use was found for it. Thus many operators have tended to fit applications and services around the technology and not vice versa. This is despite there being an evident need for a successor network to the PSTN. Modern commercial factors such as globalisation, downsizing and sharp increases in data have all driven the user market for advanced infrastructure. Many were uncertain as to whether ISDN was the technology to deliver these requirements or if it was better to keep with existing technology until a network with a greater lifespan (broadband) became more broadly available. As broadband looks more distant, especially in terms of its penetration in to all layers of the socio-economic strata, economic operators are currently utilising ISDN as a means for delivering more advanced applications/services.

As the network starts to become a true corporate resource, so the desire for its increased efficiency and effectiveness becomes a more prominent commercial issue. Changing business practices, such as economising over travel and the emergence of home offices, require more immediate solutions than broadband can currently deliver. Though it may be a transitory network, ISDN is being utilised to solve business requirements which cannot afford to wait until broadband becomes the norm. Indeed as compression technologies become more available, so commercial fears about investing in a technology with a perceptibly limited shelf life may subside.

The use of these drivers is pivotal to the commercial success of ISDN. Demand will only really exhibit its own internal dynamism when the applications of CPEs associated with the technology are able to appeal to the mass market. ISDN's market has been retarded by the perceived lack of a 'killer application',[8] the generic usage of the technology that will enable it to attain and sustain the desired critical mass for the ISDN market to mature (Bubley 1994). In seeking this 'killer application' many PTOs have sought to establish forums to bring together application developers and users with the aim of developing applications software that genuinely adds to enterprise functionality. In practice ISDN roll-out is not being driven by a single killer application but by a range of applications such as teleworking and LAN interconnection. These have provoked the take-up of the technology as the needs of users have become increasingly sophisticated.

The development of 'killer applications' was inevitably hindered by the incompatibility of national networks, a feature which inevitably increased the pressure for standardisation. The drift towards common standards will inevitably breathe further life into the technology, especially within the corporate network market. As networks internationalised so applications increasingly started to offer potential for fuller commercial exploitation. The development of such applications/services[9] is enabling enterprises of all sizes to derive greater functionality and value added from the network and proves the relevance of ISDN to all aspects of the corporate telecommunications market. As many SMEs are not able to develop private networks, ISDN offers the functionality of advanced networks as and when needed and avoids the costs associated with a dedicated network.[10]

The initial focus upon the market development of TEN-ISDN will be centred upon using it to develop effective pan-European and global enterprise networks. To this end many of the emerging global carriers are offering ISDN as part of their package. Much of this is the response of the PTOs to maintain their dominant position within the service market in what is a rapidly changing regulatory environment.

One would perhaps expect ISDN-compatible equipment to be much more expensive than its analogue counterparts due to greater complexity and functionality. This has been compounded by the failure to develop successful commercial applications/services and common standards. Such issues have meant that the actual benefit from investing in this technology proved initially marginal. This situation was not helped by the absence of the aforementioned economies of scale in CPE production, a fact compounded by the lack of commitment by PTOs to the technology. It is estimated that even if ISDN and analogue circuits were at parity the cost of ISDN equipment would have doubled the price of the technology.[11] Given the limited additional benefit traditionally available there was evidently little incentive to adopt ISDN.

Over more recent times there has been an increased take-up, in part due to increased involvement by PTOs in marketing ISDN. In addition rising personal computer penetration and lower tariffs have helped market development. Many states have used these lower tariffs to drive up demand for the technology, thereby giving users incentives to seek solutions through ISDN. Despite such market-creating measures some PTOs have fallen foul of the regulatory authorities which have claimed that the lower tariffs amount to predatory pricing.[12] Overall ISDN is starting to emerge from being a technology to a solution for enterprises.

Within a nationally dominated forum for the development of the technology, the establishment TEN-ISDN was largely secondary to the creation of a narrow indigenous service.[13] Given the development of ISDN as a technology to support the emerging network economy, such a stance is increasingly counter-productive, both in a commercial and practical sense. By the early 1990s a number of problems were emerging that hindered the development of ISDN in Europe (Public Network Europe 1991a). These included a lack of commitment and incentive to offer interconnectable and interoperable services, the poor establishment of common standards and protocols, especially in interconnecting pre-E-ISDN networks, and the backwardness of states in honouring commitments to offer ISDN interconnect. As liberalisation has proceeded, so incentives to establish multi-lateral forums for interconnect have started to grow. As a result, parochialism in ISDN grew increasingly redundant as a tool of network planning as it simply did not make commercial sense.

It is within the market context that the strategy for the development of TEN-ISDN has evolved. The aim is to overcome market deficiencies to create a critical mass to develop the network in a manner that supports the broad objectives of Europe's industrial competitiveness strategy. Initially many actions are designed to support the development of common EU-wide applications, by aiding access to the network for both suppliers and users, and facilitating the conditions for the development of a common market for terminals. This requires the development of common standards and programmes that facilitate the development of commercial and socio-cultural applications. It is hoped that these measures in combination should speed the commercial roll-out of the network into all parts of the EU economic space.

The EU's keenness to push the socio-cultural applications of TEN-ISDN is based upon establishing the necessary precursors of shifts to the information society. Given funding constraints, such priorities will inevitably require the support of the private sector. Clearly operators will not provide services that are uncommercial or have a premium of risk attached to them. Leaving the finance totally up to the market risks endangering the other priorities of telecom-TENs

70

by feasibly denying access to all social groups and regions and creating a split between information have and have-nots. If they are to remove this threat, any socio-cultural applications have to prove their worth before network owners will deliver them. The EU has produced a number of schemes which seek to prove the commercial and practical feasibility of these services (see later). The Commission hopes that the end point of such initiatives will be the holistic delivery of the socially and economically valuable services and applications solely via commercial operators, though this does remain an ideal scenario.

DEVELOPMENT OF E-ISDN

The EU's policy to stimulate the development of a market for ISDN is to overcome perceived market failure in the establishment of this technology on a Europe-wide basis. It has sought to stimulate a holistic perspective on the establishment of TEN-ISDN by European PTOs and other parts of the tele-communications industry by providing the impetus to co-ordinate actions within common forums, standard bodies and other forms of multilateral action. TEN-ISDN is in no small part a co-ordinative policy, pushing the market developers to act in what is perceived to be the common interest. There is perhaps no greater expression of this than the moves to develop a standardised form of the technology.

The development of ISDN as a TEN began as a series of bilateral inter-connection agreements signed between a number of PTOs. The EU has sought to replace bilateral forms of interconnection with multilateral forms of network integration. The shift to multilateralism also seeks to give a common general direction to network development and management. It is within this general framework that TEN-ISDN emerges. Action had been based upon rendering interoperable national standards rather than adopting common standards and protocols. Therefore full harmonious service offering was lacking. While standardisation has proceeded, the application in terms of common standard offerings has been slow. Gradually the bilateral forum for the develop of cross-border ISDN needs to be replaced by a common stance if the network is to develop as a TEN.

Table 4.1 indicates the progress to date in the implementation of E-ISDN standards. The formation of a common standard seeks to overcome the frag-mentation derived from the national dominance of network development and provide the basis for its universal coverage across the European space. The commitment to a common standard by PTOs and other bodies was due more to commercial reasons than any desire to upgrade public networks. The develop-ment of a common standard offered many more marketing opportunities. The Commission hopes that this commercial pressure spills over beyond commercial markets into holistic network development.

The development of ISDN as a European standard has been pushed since 1984 in recognition of growing interaction and rising interdependence between

Table 4.1 EU-wide access to E-ISDN

| | 1992 | | 1994 | | 1996 | |
	BRA	*PRA*	*BRA*	*PRA*	*BRA*	*PRA*
Belgium	n/a	n/a	100	100	100	100
Denmark	100	100	100	100	100	100
France	>10	>10	90	90	100	100
Germany						
West	100	100	100	100	100	100
East	>20	>20	60	60	100	100
Greece	#	#	#	#	#	#
Ireland	>8	>34	40	45	50	60
Italy	>20	>20	70	70	100	100
Luxemburg	CITY	CITY	100	100	100	100
Holland	*	*	100	100	100	100
Portugal						
TP	50	50	100	100	100	100
TLP	10	10	50	100	100	100
Spain	>20	>20	40	80	100	100
UK						
BT	40	10	100	100	100	100
Mercury						

Source: Commission of the European Communities, 1993a.
Notes:
BRA = Basic Rate Access
PRA = Primary Rate Access
# In 1993/94 the technology was available in two provinces and gradually being extended to seven by 1995.
* Limited to 30 cities.

national networks. This was in response to the need to develop a network with harmonious functionality across the EU based upon existing technology and led to the Council's recommendation[14] for co-ordination in the introduction of ISDN. This sought to create specific technical standards on ISDN, co-ordinate national policies to aid interconnection, set targets for the coverage of the technology and seek to remove incompatibilities derived from tariffing differences. Despite this initiative, progress towards the introduction of the common standard slipped.

Within the 1986 recommendation the route to E-ISDN was co-ordinative with member states volunteering, as an expression of mutual interest, to render interoperable and interconnected national networks. This was based upon a common concern that subscriber access should be updated to all users, though in practice take-up would be greater among professional/business users than the residential sector. The recommendation detailed certain services and equipment that should be interoperable by 1988. The issue of tariffs was left to the states, although a broad recognition was that pricing had to reflect a level that would facilitate the market to develop a critical mass. This evolutionary path to a set of common standards required a renewed commitment to the technology by states reflecting the political impetus that Europe was putting behind a common network. The issue of compliance was more commercial than compulsion.

The co-ordinative approach was enhanced in 1989[15] as a further response to the SEM initiative. This statement reflected more broadly the industrial policy concerns inherent within the development of E-ISDN. Evidently this was an environment where liberalisation of telecommunications was starting on a European basis. The Commission felt that this strengthened the case for stronger co-ordination of the means of mass delivery of advanced services. Within the framework of ETSI (see below), the development of ISDN was broadened beyond the PTOs and administrations to include equipment manufacturers and others as a means of pushing, as a matter of urgency, the development of a common standard. Such advances were a matter of common commercial concern. Consequently, universality issues were not at the forefront of the standardisation process. The slippage of the original recommendation was a pivotal factor in the desire for renewed activity in this area. More important was the fact that the telecommunications environment had changed since the EU's initial action and the shift towards TEN-ISDN needed to reflect this. Already this was taking place, no matter how half-heartedly, within the Memorandum of Understanding (MoU) on ISDN (see below). The resolution reflected the desire that the original ties needed to be strengthened in the light of slippage of existing commitments, the SEM and the growing evidence of communication bottlenecks.[16]

Though there was no purposeful attempt to develop TEN-ISDN, action by the PTOs under a number of forums and agreements (see below) was a step in this direction. Two phenomena are important in pushing the development of E-ISDN, as a precursor of TEN-ISDN. The first was the formation of ETSI as a common forum within which network integration could be mutually agreed; second, the Memorandum of Understanding (MoU) signed by PTOs to develop an interconnected and interoperable network within a specified time-span. Both of these schemes had direct Community influence. ETSI was set up as a response to the process of liberalisation within Europe and its consequences for the integration of networks. The MoU was developed at the suggestion of the European Commission to PTOs in the late 1980s. These forums create a series of pre-competitive interrelationships within which ISDN can, as an expression of mutual interest, develop in an harmonious fashion.

ETSI

Initially the co-ordination for the development of ISDN was based on the work carried out by SOG-T (Senior Official Group-Telecommunications). This led to the decision to produce a series of ISDN interfaces, features and services on a pan-European basis. The formation of common standards was given added impetus by the creation of ETSI in 1988. Its initial success was to enable

E-ISDN to be commercially exploited by 1992. After 1992 standards were frozen up to the end of 1995 to ensure a period of stability and consolidation in the development of E-ISDN compatible networks in Europe. This commitment to E-ISDN was reinforced with the prominence devoted to it in the initial stages of the EII.

ETSI provides the framework for the migration of incompatible national offerings towards a common norm. The work towards standardisation is complex, involving 180 different standards. Once all the standards needed for the initial development of E-ISDN were agreed, they were to be utilised to complement the development and success of the MoU (see below). Work is ongoing to ensure that all networks, both public and private, are compatible with the E-ISDN standard and that the network of networks that will form the TEN-ISDN evolves to stress the common concerns of interconnection and interoperability.

As a multilateral forum ETSI performs a careful balancing act in reflecting the broad interests inherent within ISDN development. The cost of adopting new standards inevitably means states have an interest in defending their version of the technology. This highlights that ETSI often has to reflect national industrial policy decisions in the standardisation process. Each state would inevitably like to minimise the disturbance to its network in progress to TEN-ISDN. This can often result in protracted disputes, notably in the case of applications programming interface (see below), which can slow the standardisation process and inhibit the development of TEN-ISDN. In addition, the focus of ETSI upon public networks has led to a large number of private networks being incompatible with these common standards. Consequently, focus is now directed towards removing this anomaly in the development of TENs.

The main standardisation effort for the development of TEN-ISDN will be towards the specification of more of the applications required by users, many of which are software dependent. Given the diverse nature of the market, ETSI will have to deal with assorted and often incompatible market demands. This is very much a feature of an environment where national interests desire minimal adjustment of domestic ISDN in the move towards interoperability and interconnection. Such issues will, and indeed have, slowed down the standardisation process.

MEMORANDUM OF UNDERSTANDING

In 1989 the CEPT agreed a Memorandum of Understanding (MoU),[17] in part at the request of the European Commission, for the commencement of E-ISDN services on a pan-European basis by 1992; the aim being to achieve early economies of scale and lower the risks associated with the marketability of this technology. The MoU agreed to make uniformly available a wide range of facilities and services such as primary and basic access, 64 Kbit/s unrestricted bearer service and more than twenty supplementary services. The MoU underlines a number of imperatives, namely developing generic services, stimulating the growth of new activities and employment inducing applications, expanding the market for information services by developing public and private sector applications and ensuring terminal interoperability and interconnection.

Initially representatives from twenty states committed themselves to making E-ISDN available in at least one region of their state by the deadline specified. This was seen as a precursor of full interconnection over time. By and large, the renewed commitment by PTOs (reflected within the MoU) highlights the desire of operators to use the technology to service lucrative enterprise networks. Further to support the MoU, IMIMG[18] has introduced supplementary services to exploit the commercial potential of E-ISDN to enterprises.[19]

The MoU seeks to use ETSI-defined standards to promote the roll-out of the network from the more technologically advanced states into the rest of the EU. Despite a last minute rush to honour their commitments, the MoU's objectives were broadly met by the PTOs. At the end of 1993 Euro-ISDN was launched for professional and residential users. Despite this success some states were still lagging behind in the introduction of E-ISDN. Luxemburg did not launch an E-ISDN service until March 1994, by which time the Greeks had only started a trial service.[20]

E-ISDN and the terminal market

The development of E-ISDN aims to provide the basis for the development of a pan-European equipment market. Equipment manufactured to E-ISDN standards will be able to function from any compatible connection. The degree to which the Euro-wide equipment market develops depends upon the migration paths of the respective PTOs (see below), as well as the demand for the applications offered. The reluctance to adopt ISDN reflects the maturity of the system and ongoing technological changes which may render it redundant in a few years. Therefore large-scale investment is frequently still risky. Some may continue to use advanced analogue technology modems[21] until broadband technology becomes more widely available and cost effective.

The development of a common set of protocols should allow for the establishment of a more competitive and dynamic market for terminals. The fragmented national equipment markets were not large enough to allow terminal manufacturers to create specialised terminals for each country. Thus economies of scale in production were elusive and the price of CPE remained unnecessarily high. PTOs, having invested heavily in their network, had incentives to defend their own version of ISDN from challengers as a means of minimising the reorientation costs involved in meeting common standards. As a consequence common standardisation was slow, leading to the prognosis that the technology was a failure. In the USA the market was larger, allowing the unique protocols developed by manufacturers to be more effectively justified.

The Commission's desire for a common terminals market rests upon the introduction of competition within this sector based upon pre-agreed standards. E-ISDN is therefore important in opening the European market for information technology and in accelerating the achievement of greater synergies in the development of terminal equipment. This is expected to provide the basis for greater success for EU-based CPE manufacturers on the global stage.

The development of a common market for equipment has been aided by the development of NETs.[22] NETs allow national regulators to approve telecom products for Europe-wide connection. These NETs are designed to replace CTRs.[23] NETs allow vendors to get type approval in one state as a precursor for selling this equipment across the EU.[24] Generally the development of NETs should aid the establishment of EU-wide interoperability.

In terms of terminal equipment for E-ISDN, the standardisation progress has been notoriously slow.[25] Many of the forecast dates for the development of standards have slipped markedly. Part of this was due to the relatively poor funding situation in which ETSI found itself. Despite additional funds to ensure that political commitments were met with regard to E-ISDN, progress has still been sluggish. This has resulted in substantial criticism of ETSI by many equipment manufacturers. Part of the delay, it is claimed by many equipment manufacturers, stem from the way in which ETSI functions, making the standardisation process protracted.

A further problem in the development of E-ISDN has been the strategy for the applications programming interface.[26] Two competing standards were fighting to be the common standard: the German Common ISDN Applications Programming Interface (CAPI) and the French Programming Communication Interface (PCI). ETSI has adopted the CAPI. PCI was initially approved by ETSI, backed by FT and over 20 French equipment manufacturers. This was later dropped in favour of CAPI which was developed by a German-based working group that includes DT and around 100 other companies and has over a quarter of a million users across Europe. ETSI is not allowed to have two standards but with the dominance of the German equipment it was felt that standards had to reflect market realities, not some political compromise. Most equipment manufacturers, notably Novell, IBM and Microsoft, have software that is compatible with CAPI rather than PCI. The gradual acceptance of E-ISDN is leading to market entry by an increased number of terminal suppliers. New products are entering this segment of the market and new services such as compression and virtual services are increasing the capabilities and functionality available from the network.

The migration to E-ISDN

The development of ISDN has led to a gradual route for the migration away from national standards towards E-ISDN (see Table 4.2). This migration path has been driven largely by commercial pressure rather than any coherent

Table 4.2 Migration to E-ISDN

State	Offering national ISDN until:	Offering E-ISDN from:
Belgium	end 1994	1993
Denmark	only E-ISDN	January 1992
France	upgrade	December 1993
Germany	2000	1993
Greece	—	early 1994
Eire	—	December 1993
Italy	November 1993	November 1993
Luxemburg	—	early 1994
Netherlands	1998	June 1993
Portugal	only E-ISDN	end June 1992
Spain	end 1993	end 1993
UK	2000	October 1993

Source: Commission of the European Communities (1994h). From the Fourth Annual ISDN Progress Report (COM(94)81).

industrial strategy. For example, France has introduced Euro-Numeris to replace its existing Numeris service in direct response to user pressure. A similar though longer term strategy is being adopted by Germany. In the UK, BT has adapted both its major ISDN services to be compatible with the common standards. The perceived success of E-ISDN (and its increasingly widespread adoption) is removing 'islands of ISDN' and PTOs are gradually replacing them with an integrated network of networks.

The progress of migration to E-ISDN raises two major issues. First there is the choice of strategy by which the new standards are adopted. Either an evolutionary reorientation occurs via a series of upgrades or a parallel approach to network development is offered allowing national and European ISDN systems to co-exist for a transitional period. Second, there is the question of the interlinkages and relative functionality between the existing network and E-ISDN; notably whether the new standardised services can be accessed by equipment defined by national standards and the degree of functionality of E-ISDN relative to the existing network.

Across all states the migration path has been uneven. Some, notably Austria, have shifted straight to common standards. Others, notably France and Germany, have pursued a more gradual line due to the transition costs determined by national standards. Others are slowly pushing the roll-out of E-ISDN, frequently as a new service based upon a large centre of population. Inevitably the cohesion states (notably Greece) have lagged in developing the network and commercial services based upon the technology. The states that are new to ISDN have been able to establish integrated networks from day one; the traditionally more technologically advanced states face a longer period of transition. As a consequence, over the short term, differing service levels and the incompatibilities of ISDN switches will remain. These will generally be replaced as the equipment cycle necessitates network renewal. Too often telecommunication administrations sought to establish interfaces with the network that reflected the needs of important national champions rather than focusing upon user requirements. In 1996, under the nationally orientated system of development, some 58 per cent of basic access and 51 per cent of primary access were country specific (CEC 1996).

BT's path towards the common standard has been largely user led. The choice of national or European standard is basically a user decision that allows these networks to co-exist. Thus E-ISDN will take off when there is a sufficiently large user base for the international network to attain some form of dynamism. When the user base of the national network shrinks below a certain unsustainable size, then BT will start to push users towards the international standard. Thus network externalities and the attainment of critical mass, as opposed to any direct assistance, is pushing migration towards common standards in the UK. Other states have used more persuasive methods. For example, DT has promoted migration via the use of preferential tariffs for E-ISDN.

States that adopted E-ISDN as the norm, without the necessary migration from a national standard, have found themselves in somewhat of a quandary. For most of them, for example Eire, Austria and Spain, the adoption of this technology has coincided with a time when most states are planning to move to broadband networking. Consequently the appropriateness of this migration has been questioned when a move direct to broadband might be more appropriate. Aside from this, most states where there was a national version of the technology have tended to follow an evolutionary path. An interesting case is the Netherlands, that has a version of the technology modelled upon German standards; there was a degree of dependence by the Dutch in their migration strategy to reflect any decisions made by Germany to adopt E-ISDN standards.

Much of this progression is derived from the successful development of prioritised applications. In many ways the designation of ISDN as a TEN was a natural progression from the ETSI standardisation work and was important in providing a holistic framework for PTOs to bring together differing ISDN implementation plans under a single theme.

EU SUPPORT FOR TEN-ISDN

Progress towards TEN-ISDN has always possessed some form of implicit Community support. The Community assisted in many of the initiatives leading to the development and roll-out of the E-ISDN standards. Much of this support was designed to complement the market-led development of ISDN as a TEN in the belief that once the market for the technology is in place and a critical mass is achieved it should develop in a manner compatible with the attainment of the EU's policy objectives. It is already evident that such a strategy needs further support from the public sector. This can be passive, in terms of re-regulation, or more active, in the provision of direct support to network development. Both of these have been key features in the strategy to develop TEN-ISDN.

Initially the aim of TEN-ISDN is to consolidate the existing movement, within the EU, towards the harmonised introduction of ISDN. The Council resolution of 5 June 1992, for the development of ISDN as an EU-wide telecommunications infrastructure, sought to reinforce trends towards interoperability between Europe's respective ISDN networks. As a result, a working group TEN-ISDN,[27] which included a wide variety of interested parties, set out to define a basic TEN-ISDN based upon E-ISDN standards. Three basic measures for the development of TEN-ISDN were sought (Rietbroek 1993):

- providing velocity to E-ISDN introduction plans;
- support for the development of end-to-end telematic services;[28]
- measures to assist in terminal availability.

The establishment of TEN-ISDN as a policy measure is designed to utilise the powers given to the Commission within the Maastricht Treaty to add impetus to the EU's ISDN development. The TEN-Telecom[29] initiative aims to set the parameters for the expression of this power by ensuring that any support given is in line with the Treaty's provisions. TEN-Telecom seeks to reflect the user-driven requirements for the commercial roll-out of networks. Consequently, the priority is to stimulate applications that overcome the hesitancy of potential users to utilise new services and of the private sector to invest in advanced technology. Thus a Commission priority is to break the vicious cycle of underinvestment that has limited the development of ISDN networks within the EU. Within TEN-Telecom, ISDN is a testing ground technology to stimulate demand for existing infrastructure. As users get more sophisticated this should create the commercial desire to invest in ever more advanced networks.

For the period 1993 to 1997 the Community adopted an ISDN development plan which, by stressing key themes within the TENs initiative, seeks to embrace their holistic growth by eliminating bottlenecks to interconnection in the implementation of E-ISDN, ensuring basic interoperability of telematic services, plotting the migration of existing public and private applications towards the common standard (E-ISDN) and ensuring the compatibility of CPE. To meet these objectives limited amounts of community funding have been forthcoming much of which has been used for preliminary studies.[30]

It is already clear that there is a large financing gap between what the Commission wants the private sector to pay for and what it will actually invest in practice. Community funding for TEN-ISDN seeks to close this financing gap by increasing the commercial appeal of TEN-ISDN and associated applications and services. The Commission estimates that it will cost some ECU6 billion to provide access to all business subscribers,[31] which is the initial stage of network development, though this figure tends to exaggerate the cost as that assumes all states are starting from zero penetration which is clearly not the case.

Table 4.3 indicates the funding available from the Community budget to support projects within the domain of Telecom-TENs. Support for TEN-ISDN from this budget line is a fraction of the funding required. The intention is to use these monies to support projects which are likely to attract sustained private sector finance beyond the period over which EU funding is available. Thus the EU's prioritised applications and generic services need to prove their potential marketability before Community support may be forthcoming. This finance is also to be used to ensure that those services and applications utilising TEN-ISDN as a delivery platform are compatible with the anticipated migration to broadband networks.

Table 4.3 EU funding for telecom-TENs
(millions of ECU)

1996	1997	1998	1999
30	35	77	114

Source: Commission of the European Communities, 1995b

Other forms of assistance available include the structural funds, the Fourth Framework, the EIB or the EIF. Many of these are focused upon digitalisation of networks for the purposes of regional development and cohesion (see below). Telecom-TENs projects are not research projects, though they are inevitably interlinked to schemes such as telematics. Ultimately this funding is designed to enhance the spatial and social availability of the network via assorted market creating initiatives.

Table 4.4 Priorities of TEN-ISDN support

Areas of action	Projects of common interest	Interoperability measures
• Infrastructure • Trans-frontier applications and services • Projects promoting ISDN usage • End-to-end compatibility of certain telematic services and accompanying equipment • Awareness of E-ISDN	• Bottlenecks • Specifying technical requirements • Action plans • Validation of certain functions • Assessment of results • Identifying needs of SMEs • Plot migration to E-ISDN	• Software and associated prototypes • Interoperable solutions identified by Euro label • Standards • Testing • Disseminating results • Awareness of interoperability

Source: Adapted from European Commission information

Table 4.4 highlights the broad areas where EU action seeks to complement and enhance market forces to ensure the network develops in the desired manner. Clearly many of these focus upon the ambition to broaden E-ISDN via its deployment and development by commercial operators. The end point of all these actions is to ensure that access to TEN-ISDN is non-discriminatory in terms of price and functionality and its value is realised within a broad range of user groups.

The projects of common interest tend to be characterised by the nature of the fact that they act as impediments to the establishment of a Common Information Area. Consequently the focus is upon assisting the mobility of information via addressing the concerns of bottlenecks, application incompatibilities and conformity to common standards.

The largely passive network management role taken by the EU in the development of TEN-ISDN reflects its relative impotence in terms of funding. This action is complemented by its regulatory role which seeks to develop TEN-ISDN as a competitive response to actual and potential market entry (Stehmann 1995). EU action has also sought to establish industry-wide forums as a means of increasing the marketability and adoption of E-ISDN compatible networks. Such forums[32] are likely to be all-embracing, including not only PTOs but also manufacturers and users.

The development of partnerships in the realisation of the network, both within and between private and public sectors, partially reflects the Commission's scepticism towards the concept of competition delivering TEN-ISDN. Without some form of pre-competitive agreement, it feels too much competition too soon would retard TEN-ISDN. The Commission also feels that competition between manufacturers has led to the telematics gap (see below); the aim to offer differentiated services has led to the emergence of incompatible networks. Competition is not perceived as being undesirable. Commercial pressure will ultimately dictate the form of the network. The task is to manage this network in a manner that is compatible with the broader policy objectives. The importance of the EU is in pinpointing mutuality of interests inherent within the network and in promoting the development of public–private partnerships and forums to address these issues.

Ensuring access to E-ISDN-based facilities and the full geographic coverage of a standardised network remain explicit objectives of the Commission's strategy for TEN-ISDN. As a consequence, integral to the development of ISDN has been the use of the technology to promote its broader utilisation for commercial and socio-cultural purposes. In the case of commercial services, the application of the principles of Open Network Provision (ONP) has been applied to the network, while socio-cultural concerns are represented by the active promotion of ISDN as a tool for the delivery of telematic services. Both of these concerns are indicative of the EU's network management role in the development of TEN-ISDN.

ISDN and ONP: pushing for commercial access

The extension of ONP to ISDN technology seeks to promote harmonised service offerings over a common European network. This requires broader adoption of

E-ISDN, though access should be just as liberal to national ISDN systems. A further key concern is to meet interoperability and interconnection requirements as a precursor for these harmonised service offerings. Giving all relevant service providers access to this network is a fundamental component in attaining and sustaining the commercial roll-out of ISDN. Though the application of ONP to ISDN is not a prime policy focus, its importance lies in its perceived ability to deliver more advanced services and CPEs at tariffs which can attain and sustain a critical mass for this technology. Consequently, access of this nature is perceived by the EU to be central to promoting the greater utilisation of the technology by both sides of the market (Ovum 1995).

The liberalisation of the VANs market created pressure upon service providers to use ISDN technology to deliver greater functionality to a largely business market. Despite a maturing of the market for the technology, access to the ISDN by broader socio-economic groupings for whom there is as yet no proven effective demand will tend to be neglected by commercial operators. The servicing of these groups may not be an issue for transnational service providers that are leading the commercial roll-out of ISDN, but is of importance to member states and the EU in promoting economic development.

ISDN and telematics: importance of ISDN as a socio-economic infrastructure

Much of the development of TEN-ISDN is linked to the increased consumption of telematic applications/services that serve directly to complement the economic and social priorities of the EU. The development of telematics services is an important part of broadening the use of ICTs into previously excluded areas of the socio-economic strata. The market has already shown that it can utilise ISDN to provide a range of services for commercial usage. Action by the EU in this area aims partially to determine that the information and functionality delivered by TEN-ISDN, with regards to generic services and specific applications, is of relevance and economic value to citizens and SMEs.[33]

Consequently, the ultimate policy aim is to establish a series of key commercial and socio-cultural applications. The intention is to utilise these applications and services and exploit their commercial potential to meet universality concerns. A further focus of policy is to break the vicious cycle of network underdevelopment which has led to the 'telematics gap', which is a direct expression of market failure and arises from a perceived absence of end-to-end user, non-voice services within this sector. Part of the problem of telematic services is disputes over who is responsible for their provision and incompatibilities resulting from a multi-vendor environment. The Commission[34] blames this deficiency upon competition between manufacturers of terminals. It is felt that excessive competition breeds a desire to produce differentiated equipment that limits interoperability of networks.[35]

While telematics technology is technologically feasible, its deployment is hindered by the uncertainty that exists over demand, a fact which deters investment in the technology and its accompanying infrastructure. As a consequence a key objective is to utilise the funding available for the development of telecom-TENs to breed an increased familiarity with telematics delivered by TEN-ISDN. The application programmes aim to take the technology to its starting point, enabling the development of experimental services, an assessment of feasibility and the broader acceptance and realisation of potentialities in the targeted sectors.[36] The aim is to push for a convergence between the requirements of society and commerce by stressing policy themes such as cohesive development, environmental management and investment in human capital. These are perceived as necessary prerequisites for the desired levels of commercial investment to be forthcoming.

Despite the potential for these services there has been scant interest in developing applications related to socio-cultural concerns. This leads to a partial conclusion that market failure for these applications is deeply entrenched and that the EU is trying to create a market for a series of applications and services that, over the short term at least, are simply not marketable. However, it is too soon to conclude that such failure is indicative of government failure and a poor understanding of the differences between the social and commercial potential of telematics.

ISDN AND REGIONAL DEVELOPMENT: SCHEMES FOR COHESION

The EU feels that, overall, advances in communications networks will have a positive effect on regional development. Consequently, cohesion is an important issue in the development of TEN-ISDN (Commission of the European Communities 1990b). To this end it has initiated schemes to promote investment upon network digitalisation in peripheral regions.

ISDN is seen as a tangible way of reducing spatial disparities by exploiting the potentialities of existing infrastructure.[37] A primary focus is to close the telematics gap, which is perceived to be worse when analysed within a core–periphery dichotomy. Many of the initiatives followed by the EU seek to address this spatial telematics gap. Any benefits to a region from digitalisation will only be derived from the quality of the services and information provided over them. Telematics is seen as a way in which the roll-out of ISDN to these regions can feed through into improved economic performance. These concerns have been reflected in the Commission's two major initiatives to promote advanced telecommunications in the regions, STAR and Télématique; STAR was infrastructure led, while Télématique focused upon improving the value added of the network developed under its forerunner.

STAR (Special Telecommunications Action for Regional Development)

Initiated in 1986, the STAR scheme contributed ECU1.5 billion up to 1991 to promote investment, awareness and sectoral applications of advanced narrow-band networks in the peripheral areas of the EU. A key aim was to add velocity to the process of network digitalisation in the less developed areas of the European economy. Consequently some 80 per cent of the 300 projects supported were infrastructure related.

The Commission that claims the STAR initiative has been successful in promoting its aims (Commission of the European Communities 1992). In terms of digitalisation, STAR funding has contributed some 5 to 10 per cent of national investment, largely PTO led. STAR has also contributed funding to establishing inter-regional and international digital transmission highways using broadband techniques. The installation of digital infrastructure in the regions, to prepare for E-ISDN, represented some 37.6 per cent of the STAR budget. At least 15 per cent was focused on promoting the demand for and supply of telecommunications services.

STAR had an underlying objective of ensuring an integrated market for E-ISDN by specifying that all schemes supported had to use the common standard and obey the EU's ONP recommendations. STAR enabled the EU to have direct influence over the development of networks to ensure they complemented trends elsewhere. The infrastructure initiatives existed alongside actions to promote advanced services within these regions. Evidently access promotion is only as effective as the desirability and use derived from the network. Consequently the services had to be developed as a means of sustaining the investment in the infrastructure once the scheme ended.[38]

In specific ways STAR is likely to have speeded up the roll-out of ISDN in a number of areas of the EU. While STAR kickstarted the process, the funding available meant that ultimately it would be limited in its success. Further action, largely led by the private sector with public sector support, was required. Such commercial support was frequently not forthcoming. Its major effect was to enable PTOs to bring forward investment plans in digital infrastructure. Although beneficial, constraints upon enterprises, for example their ability to borrow for network development, tended to diminish its impact. The experiences of the impact of STAR in a number of states is varied.[39] Many say[40] that it is too soon to say if STAR had an impact in regional development. In the case of Northern Ireland, STAR more directly assisted the performance of larger organisations rather than SMEs. In Spain the persistently high price of terminals limited its effectiveness.

Télématique

Télématique, approved in 1991 and designed to run until 1993 with resources of ECU200 million, was the successor initiative to STAR. The general themes of the initiative are similar to those in STAR: to aid access to advanced services by SMEs; introduce data communications to users in the public sector; and improve access to data communication networks within the remoter parts of the EU. In all affected states, the aim was to utilise the digitalisation programme of STAR to develop more advanced services for those who would have otherwise been denied access. This reflected the fact that whereas STAR focused upon infrastructure, Télématique sought to be more content orientated. Most if not all member states that benefited from STAR recognised its importance in reducing the infrastructure gap by addressing differences in access to telematic services between core and periphery.[41]

Over the longer term the impact of such schemes was to ensure that the peripheral areas do not emerge as a series of information have-nots in the evolving information society. This has been reflected in successive actions since the end of Télématique. Despite the perceptible successes it is unlikely that such schemes will remove differences in network quality between the core and the periphery.

More recent schemes reflect a belief among many regions that access to ISDN may be yesterday's issue. Concern is now about access to broadband networking. This technology rather than ISDN is seen by peripheral areas as increasingly pivotal to their generally inferior levels of technological development. The preoccupation with TEN-ISDN, especially in cohesion terms, is an attempt to fill a regional gap in establishing access to some form of advanced networking in these areas. In practice, better access to ISDN will not ultimately stop these regions falling behind. Market failures cannot really be remedied as the potential for advanced services in these regions remains elusive. The delivery of broadband to peripheral areas is unfeasible commercially without greater quantities of public sector support.

The concerns of not falling further behind the core, in terms of ISDN's successor networks, are reflected in schemes to meet network requirements of the periphery. A Memorandum of Understanding (MoU) between six regions[42] has been signed which reflects their common interests in not being excluded from the advent of such developments. The initiative, entitled the IRISI,[43] seeks to develop a number of advanced applications in selected fields, notably telematics for SMEs, healthcare and other social applications and public administration.

This network of regions has priorities that are strongly parallel to those of the EU and consists of all areas that qualify for aid under the structural funds. The network seeks to enable them to share their collective knowledge with regard to research carried out within their respective geographic areas. By exploiting EU funding and inter-regional synergies, this network seeks to allow them to reverse their relative position by adopting these technologies and has managed to achieve financial support from the EU to enable it to establish itself. While such an initiative is innovative, the diversity of interests within it may mean that priority setting in terms of action may be fraught with dispute.

This action is complemented by other initiatives from the structural funds that have sought to increase the rate of network digitalisation in the remotest parts of the EU. These initiatives once again seek to promote digitalisation as a means of increasing the consumption of telematic services. This is linked to projects such as BIRD[44] which seeks to develop a strategy for the application of telematics in rural areas.

Despite these initiatives, the access to E-ISDN in peripheral areas still lags behind the rest of the EU. Many of these states now have universal coverage but the functionality derived is still behind core regions. While schemes do exist to utilise the technology in these regions, enterprises in the core have inherent advantages due to the greater density of users, a telecommunications network with more complete geographic coverage as well as a market which is technologically more mature. Although digitalisation of the network has proceeded this has not been sufficient to overcome technological disparities. While the periphery accepts and utilises ISDN, many parts of the core are already moving to broadband networks.

These handicaps mean that investment in ISDN will do little to alter the relative position of these regions. While the network economy offers potential for more dispersed growth, the absence of advanced networks and sophisticated users may dissipate its impact in the areas that need it most.

EXTERNAL INTEROPERABILITY OF E-ISDN

As part of the development of the EII, ETSI is seeking to push for the global interoperability of Europe's advanced networks, thereby ensuring the global functionality of the European standard.[45] The actions of the standards bodies are complemented by the emerging global carriers such as Concert and Uniworld that are offering global ISDN as part of an expanding service portfolio in response to commercial pressure.

Even before such manoeuvres, efforts were already being made to deliver global interoperability. There were a number of schemes, notably the EC–Japan Interconnection Experiment, which sought to deliver interoperability via bilateral agreement. These have now been superseded by holistic developments such as EII, which sets the global interoperability of E-ISDN within the context of the global information infrastructure.

The EU has sought to deliver true pan-European interoperability of E-ISDN by enabling non-EU states to partake in the standardisation process. The acceptance of ETSI standards has also been expanded to other states by the work of organisations such as EIB whose investment patterns in infrastructure have been strongly swayed by the desire for interoperability. Global interoperability has been further enhanced by the acceptance of ETSI standards outside Europe in the Far East, Australia, South Africa, Israel, Latin America and Indonesia. The MoU on the implementation of the Euro-ISDN protocols has been signed by all these areas.

In practice the interconnection of ISDN has not, over recent times, been a priority for major industrialised states. Instead, the emphasis has been upon the interconnection of successor networks. There have been actions within the G7 forum to ensure the interconnection and mutual development of a number of telematic services that are likely to involve global interoperability of TEN-ISDN. The global interconnection of E-ISDN has evolved from Europe's participation in assorted initiatives to deliver specific applications that offer global interoperability. The aim is to extend many of the services available under the MoU on a global basis.

TEN-ISDN AND INDUSTRIAL POLICY

Earlier sections of this chapter noted that the importance of TEN-ISDN for industrial strategy lay in two key areas: first in its role as a stepping-stone to broadband; second, in stimulating the rise of the information society by offering access to advanced networks by a broad range of user groups. An immediate consequence of this latter priority was to ensure that SMEs have access to more advanced telecommunication networks. The SMEs communication environment has undergone a rapid transformation with the advent of the SEM and TEN-ISDN was perceived as a method of supporting these requirements. Pricing these firms out of the access to more advanced telecommunications is perceived as risking long-term damage to the competitiveness of the EU economy. Access to ISDN by SMEs has been aided by sharp falls in the price of basic entry since the realisation of the MoU.[46]

The EU strategy for TEN-ISDN has been based on the French model of PTO alliances that are utilised for the development of new applications. To aid the progress of TEN-ISDN as a technology relevant to a broad range of users, DG XIII established a series of training programmes to encourage firms, especially SMEs, to utilise ISDN via the common standards. This is a shift of the priorities of the Commission away from being solely concerned with research and development towards methods of encouraging greater familiarity with the technology. To this extent the EU has sought initiatives to promote the availability of E-ISDN software, train staff in distribution and implementation of E-ISDN terminals and to utilise the network of Euro-Information centres as a forum for the creation of pilot projects.

Table 4.5 illustrates the linkage between the development of TEN-ISDN and the network management role of the EU. It highlights how such action is designed to be holistic in terms of developing TEN-ISDN as a resource across a wide range of users, as well as establishing the precursors for its commercial roll-out.

The commonality provided by TEN-ISDN allows a number of competitive advantages in terms of improved functionality beyond simple telephony, a rationalisation of CPE, improved connection to computer systems and an effective back-up for leased lines. Increasingly, ISDN is justified in terms of improving the performance of those that access it, both enterprises and workers,

Table 4.5 Network management and TEN-ISDN

Network concerns	Actions
Universality: cohesion	STAR, Télématique, digitalization of network funded by structural funds, support for national action
Universality: access	ONP, telematics initiative, training
Interconnection	MoU, ETSI, multi-annual guidance scheme, promoting industry forums, global interconnection agreements
Interoperability	Euro-ISDN, international interoperability

the applications and services delivered and the extent to which it pushes the European economy forward to more advanced forms of telecommunication networking. Already the development of E-ISDN has led to more advanced forms of networking being offered to multi-site SMEs.[47]

The increased commitment to ISDN has occurred as its potential role in the meeting of Europe's broad industrial objectives has become more fully understood. The EU aims to use the technology to push a greater familiarity with ICTs as a precursor to the onset of the information society. ISDN is a means of delivering competitive advantage without a massive renewal or investment in infrastructure to support such changes. As the market will lead the roll-out of broadband network and accompanying services, ISDN is a useful benchmark for the justification of such investment.

While ISDN, or some form of digital network, will become available to the residential market, there is currently little demand. Only when the sectors with which the residential market comes into contact on a regular basis, such as public services, start delivering information in digital format will demand be stimulated.[48] Despite this, the rising take-up of teleworking and the desire for networked PCs may enhance greater degrees of familiarity with ISDN technology, thereby increasing its penetration within the residential sector.

Matson (1987) argues that the renewed commitment to ISDN is a direct response to the new competitive environment. The development of ISDN allows the PTOs to protect their investment in copper wire. This has a consequence for ISDN as a route map for the development of IBC.[49] If Matson is correct, the desire to protect existing investments will delay the introduction of IBC. The development of ISDN as a TEN should therefore be abandoned, with the policy being focused upon a move straight to broadband and not via advanced narrowband networks.

Such a scenario can only be argued where a monopoly over networks remains intact. If this is broken then it is no longer in the interests of the PTOs to protect their investment. It is hoped that the freedom to provide network infrastructure will promote greater investment in advanced technology and infrastructure renewal. This is reflected in the logic of the conclusions of the Bangemann Report (Bangemann Group 1994) that sees a close interdependence between liberalisation and network advancement.

The importance of ISDN as a tool of industrial policy lies in its ability to offer enhanced functionality over existing infrastructure. This is important for those parts of the EU's social and economic strata for whom large-scale investment in broadband is, as yet, commercially unjustified. ISDN is therefore a stopgap using the existing infrastructure to ensure that inequalities between core and periphery and information have and have-nots do not increase. Trends within core regions and larger corporations are towards investment in fibre optic cabling, which would result in a larger gap between different users. TEN-ISDN can only limit this effect if it is taken up in sufficient quantities by the targeted user groups. Experience seems to suggest that this is some way off.

The development of TEN-ISDN does not deny the ability of states to develop broadband. What it does aim to do is to enable a minimum level of service for all parts of the EU, with everyone having access to some form of digital network. Broadband will not develop uniformly. ISDN is therefore deemed to be a suitable halfway house for advanced communications for peripheral areas and diverse user communities. ISDN may be a mid-step but commercially it is realistic, given the resources needed to develop the broadband network holistically. The mass migration of users from an analogue network straight to broadband is likely to be too large a commercial step to take at once and is therefore unlikely to encourage the investment required. It is also unlikely that the market is ready to exploit the potential of broadband. ISDN is there-fore a logical evolutionary step towards broadband, but the question is how long this step will last.

FUTURE OF TEN-ISDN

The EU is putting a lot of political capital into a technology that, first, has taken a long time to prove itself of use and, second, appears to have little long-term future. The rise of data communications within the corporate environment can feasibly be credited with the rising commercial commitment to ISDN by PTOs. The strategy for TEN-ISDN realises this fact. The main reason for it to appear within the TENs initiative is one of immediacy. ISDN can be exploited to deliver enhanced network functionality now. In addition, while the core may already be moving to fibre optic networks, this step is still some way off for many of the peripheral states.

The positioning of ISDN has also been strengthened by the political capital put in the establishment of the information society. Consequently existing technology needs to be utilised to push this along, with its associated applications and services where commercially and technologically feasible. The transitory nature of TEN-ISDN seeks to ensure full interoperability and interconnection with Europe's broadband networks. Any application/service developed to run over TEN-ISDN should be compatible with, and able to be readily transferred to, the more advanced network.

Yet the successful development of ISDN still has to overcome the market failures that have dogged its development. ISDN has given the appearance of a technology that developed before anybody had really found a use for it. As a result applications and services were designed around it rather than vice versa. As a consequence it has had to overcome large marketability problems. Past failures are likely to continue to haunt it over the coming years. The 'killer applications' are now slowly emerging with many, such as Internet access and file transfer, improving the technological development of smaller sized enterprises. In addition, the benefits in terms of the terminal market have still to be fully realised. Bubley (1994) highlights that in many cases the market is still not ready due to excessive CPE prices.

Many of the failures within ISDN can be credited to the fact that a common market for the technology was absent on a pan-European level. Although this is changing, market failures are still likely to remain. Within the shift to the information society, two further scenarios could emerge to limit the benefits of network development.[50] First, there could be a division between information have and have-nots. In many ways the strategy to deliver TEN-ISDN to a position where it is accessible to all seeks to overcome this, though differences in quality and type of information available will inevitably vary. Second, information overload could occur. Within the context of a liberalised environment for communications networks, there could be an explosion of information available to users that prevents rational and speedy decisions and dissemination of knowledge. Though the former is more likely than the latter, both scenarios contain the possibility of undermining the competitiveness of enterprises.

According to Bubley (1994: 156) 'a mentality exists that innovation is necessarily not only good but also instantly popular'. ISDN goes against this aloof attitude. In prioritising TEN-ISDN, the EU is expecting operators and users to make investments in a technology that may have a limited shelf life. Questions therefore need to be asked as to why the EU should offer commitment to a transitory technology and why operators and users should not wait until broadband comes along. In part these concerns are answered by the industrial policy themes and the importance of being seen to do something to promote the structural and social change associated with the shift to an information society.

There is hope that the development of ISDN as a TEN may prove more rational than otherwise suggested. Aside from questions of immediacy, the increased commitment shown to it by the sector has once again highlighted its increasing relevance to technologically advancing user communities. This has been highlighted by the utilisation of this technology within the ever-advancing service offerings of global carrier networks. As the information society advances, so its pertinence should extend ever further. In addition, the advent of compression technologies could mean that it may not be as transitory as is supposed. In these circumstances, the uneven development of broadband may not be as detrimental to European economic cohesion as currently believed.

CONCLUSION

The prioritisation of TEN-ISDN reflects the evolutionary path to broadband taken by the EU. Initially the aim has been to integrate national networks of ISDN and then roll it out into peripheral areas. The commercial-led development of TEN-ISDN faces a number of problems that have been inherent since its advent. One of the key failures is that it has been slow to develop killer applications that are a necessary precursor of the ISDN market to attain a critical mass.

EU action with regard to TEN-ISDN has focused upon market creation to ensure the network develops in the desired manner. To this end it has promoted standardisation, access and cohesion via a number of schemes. The wisdom of promoting a technology that has been seen as at best transitory has been called in to question. The need for advanced communications has been used as a justification for its priority status. Despite this, market failures are still likely to inhibit the development of ISDN as a true TEN. Already financing gaps are emerging; this means that access and consumption of ISDN-based services vary widely over space. Despite the significant progress of the EU towards the conditions for TEN-ISDN, doubts still exist as to whether commerce will deliver the expected benefits to all of Europe's diverse socio-economic groupings and regions.

5

TRANS-EUROPEAN TELEMATIC NETWORKS

INTRODUCTION

The development of a series of telematic applications and derivative generic services is central to the realisation of TENs. Consequently telematics represents a key priority of the EU in the promotion of telecom-TENs. Within the EU's market-led strategy, the development of network infrastructure is dependent upon a series of commercially and technologically feasible telematic applications and services. The prioritised telematic applications and services (see later) are intended to run initially over ISDN with an eventual migration to IBC envisaged over the medium to longer term.

This chapter examines the nature of telematics technology, noting its principal proposed uses and anticipated impacts. The major schemes to promote the development and deployment of telematic networks within the EU are examined. A primary focus will be the moves to establish a series of networks between Europe's administrations, which represent the initial priority of the EU with regard to telematic technology and telecom-TENs. This is followed by an examination of the promotion of telematics within the Fourth Framework Programme. Finally, the global dimension of this technology is explored.

NATURE AND DEVELOPMENT OF TELEMATICS IN EUROPE

Telematics has evolved from the integration of computer, information and telecommunication technologies. This integration offered opportunities for the development of telematic networks to improve commercial performance and social cohesion via the potential for improved information handling and manipulation. Generally a telematic network will seek to integrate:

- data creation, organisation and handling (information technology);
- data storage and processing (computer technology);
- data transportation over larger distances (telecommunications technology).

The applications of telematic technology can be broadly split into two key areas (Bangemann 1994): first, the personal/residential market which includes functions such as interactive services, video, teleshopping and other entertainment and leisure applications; second, business and socio-economic applications which seek to ensure these networks deliver value added to enterprises and improve economic performance.

France led the development of telematic technology and French was the initial language of application. The UK, the USA and Germany have also developed telematic systems, though these have tended to be less successful than Minitel, the French system. Minitel started as a residential service, but has developed the supply of business services to push its commercial evolution.

Telematic networks, within the telecom-TENs initiative, are perceptibly different from the other priority networks. They are dedicated networks defined by the applications or services that run over them. The development of telematics by the EU is linked to applications being developed across a wide social and economic spectrum to meet both specific sectoral (e.g. transport) and generic (e.g. teleworking) needs.

Telematics lies at the heart of many product, process and organisational innovations within a variety of public and private environments. The technology offers opportunities for improving the design and control of production and distribution, as well as reducing the importance of location in organisational decisions (see Chapter 2). In a global economy, telematic systems are likely to be of increased significance in terms of responses to market signals and to enable multi-site units to produce in the most efficient manner. This partly explains the perceived importance of telematics in regional development.

The benefits of the technology can be derived from a number of sources such as the 'substitution effect', as contacts are established without the need for travel, and the 'incremental effect', as new services and opportunities emerge as a result of these technological advancements. Such developments parallel the evolution of the network economy. The emergence of locationally and structurally independent enterprises or relational organisations is inevitably complemented by telematic networks (Gillespie 1993). The end point is the creation of a virtual organisation/enterprise where factors other than simple physical proximity dictate intra-firm structures.

The focus of public policy is the development of these telematic networks as a social and economic tool. Consequently the EU is prioritising applications such as teleworking, distance learning and tele-medicine. These are perceived to underline the socio-economic potential of telematic networks as well as highlighting how this technology can potentially improve economic performance by infusing advanced communications into diverse user groups.

Telematics has evident potential to strengthen economic performance by broadening access to this technology in a number of areas. In the work environment, telematics has or is likely to have a pronounced impact upon inter- and intra-corporate/organisational communication in terms of factors such as the potential for more dispersed work patterns. Telematics has also been used in the transportation sector to monitor and manage flows of traffic and overcome any consequences for economic performance and development from such phenomena.[1] Additionally the deployment of this technology also offers the potential for the spatial convergence of economic development (see later).

The evolution of telematic technology, alongside the shift to liberalisation within the sector, has tended to cause a divergence between the preference of PTOs and the EU in telematic development. The PTOs have been largely concerned with telematic applications that enable them to preserve or enhance their market position. In practice this means that these operators are frequently developing services linked to the business of large trans-national enterprises. Inevitably the development of socio-cultural applications will tend to be retarded by such concerns as operators will be focused upon effective demand and not need or socio-cultural potential.

Commercial issues may also undermine the incentives to deliver inter-connection and interoperability in the development of telematic networks. This is derived from the desire to offer differentiated applications and services with limited applicability and access. The EU noted in its fourth report (CEC 1994h) upon the development of E-ISDN that such trends have created a 'telematics gap' in Europe. Competitive forces have led to telematic services and technology developing in a fragmented and incoherent manner. Consequently, policy has highlighted the desirability of greater co-ordination, both within industry and super-national bodies, to develop these networks as TENs. This offers the possibility of overcoming concerns for market failure associated with access being linked to economic rather than social need. There has been a push by the EU to induce the commercial development, via a system of both passive and active support, of prioritised social, economic and cultural applications where they are technologically feasible and economically viable.[2]

The development of these socio-economic applications for the technology is perceived as vital to its success. History has shown that new technologies only achieve the desired growth when they become available for creative use by consumers and their servicing enterprises (Soekka 1990). The development of telematics technology is only part of the story; across Europe large differences persist in the manner in which member states produce and consume telematics services. This is important, for the socio-economic impact of this technology will be dependent upon the maturity of the telematics infrastructure and services.

TELEMATIC STRATEGIES AND PRIORITIES

The EU's telematic initiatives are an attempt to determine, in part, that the content delivered by the networks provides value added to the economy. Such benefits can be derived from improvements in economic performance or by socio-cultural enrichment. The priorities of the Commission are tending to differ markedly from those of commercial service providers. Despite this the Commission hopes to utilise this experience and technology to entice operators to become more closely involved in the development of its priority applications.

The Commission's priorities for telematics have altered as the challenges to the European economy have changed. The initial emphasis for telematic network development was as a direct aid and complement to the establishment of the Single European Market (SEM). These concerns have been overtaken by broader priorities related to competitiveness and growth in the early 1990s. The potential exists for telematics to act not only as a complement to mobility but also as a broader tool in economic regeneration and development. The anticipated flexibility induced by the development of such networks is seen as a positive factor in the growth process. This aspiration reflects the belief that the mobility of goods is less important in the information economy. In this context, mobility tends to focus upon information and its accessibility within a variety of environments.

The priorities within the White Paper (CEC 1993b) reflect the desire to establish a series of applications and services that is likely to be integral to the attainment of the EU's broad industrial policy objectives (Table 5.1). These applications and services are also perceived as having the potential to stimulate a critical mass for telematic and other advanced telecommunication networks. Such effects, the Commission feels, could offer tangible benefits to the European economy over the medium to longer term (CEC 1993e).

The relationship between services and applications is akin to that between vehicles and cargo in the transportation sector. Infrastructure is the means of mass delivery of services. Services are the means and format of applications and applications are specific utilisation of the technology. This underpins the perceived policy link of applications being formalised within services, which in turn influence the demand for infrastructure. These services (Table 5.1) are designed to diversify the applications over a given infrastructure and eventually to deliver generic appeal and marketability. The applications are testbeds for the technology which may evolve into more fully developed generic telematic services.

The EU's desire to seek to determine not only the physical infrastructures but also what is run over the networks is problematic; it is seeking to determine the content of something for which it does not pay. Already PTOs and other involved parties (such as broadcasters, IT companies and entertainment firms) have dismissed such intervention. Commercial operators will prioritise those

Table 5.1 Telematic application and service priorities in 'Growth' White Paper

Services	Applications
Electronic images	Teleworking
Electronic access to information	Links between administrations
Electronic mail	Teletraining
	Telemedicine

Source: Commission of the European Communities (1993b)

telematic networks which show the greatest commercial, not social-cultural, potential. Such differences are tending to exhibit themselves in the large financing gaps for the Commission's prioritised projects. It is already evident that Commission funding is insufficient to stimulate the commercial sector to bridge such gaps.

EUROPEAN NERVOUS SYSTEM (ENS)

The European Nervous System is a series of trans-European telematic applications which link distinct parts of the administrative structure of member states (Ridge 1994). The ENS emerged as a priority due to the challenges posed for policy and economic management by the advent of the SEM. The ENS also reflects a belief that efficient and effective administration is a co-requisite to the potential economic advantages to be derived from the SEM. The SEM bred increased interaction between administrations as each needed to manage the implications for their respective domains. Notably administrative networks were needed to administer common policies, prevent fraud and to manage increased mobility and accessibility within and between EU states. Exchange between administrations occurs at two levels: first, between the administrations of member states; second, between supranational and national bodies. This breeds interdependancies between administrations at all levels which are formalised within the ENS.

Community action is focused upon defining the common requirements for electronic information exchange and ensuring interoperability between existing administrative networks. This action seeks eventually to establish a 'virtual European administrative service' which offers the perception of a single administrative structure despite the continuation of operations on a regional, local or national level. The culmination of this action is to establish the EU as an 'enabler' by encouraging public administrations to participate in these schemes. Such efforts are complementary and are not designed to replace local applications. On the whole, they will focus upon the stimulation of services to ensure that they are ripe for commercial deployment.

While common services are not envisaged, the more frequent contact between national administrations implies the requirement of a greater harmonisation of the organisations and regulations concerned. Such a trend may bring less administered states into line with others as a means of developing standardised if not centralised procedures across the EU. The development of the ENS implies modernisation within many administrations with its accompanying efficiencies. For the development of these networks to aid competitiveness, their effects should be felt not only in terms of organisational and administrative efficiency but in the delivery of services that are of genuine use to citizens. There is frequently little or no link between the use of telematics to improve public administration and their usage to enrich public services.

Any support given by the EU is based upon the prerequisite that these projects reach a stage of development that facilitates the rapid dissemination and replication of data. The network should promote a culture of best practice which puts the focus upon achieving results that can be repeated and not on simply expanding the level of technology employed. It is hoped that a commonality of stance upon these issues can produce further savings in other areas such as procurement. The development of the ENS comes with an important precondition, namely that any project should have a firm commitment from the member state concerned. This is for practical (funding) and political (subsidiarity) purposes and leads to a problem in that the potential major funders and users of such networks, the state and its public service providers, are going through a period of fiscal retrenchment.

As with the other telematic schemes, the development of the ENS is designed to respond to user requirements. This stance reflects a desire to determine the networks' marketability and to ensure that they operate as a practical expression of evolving administrative procedures. Many states have implemented national administrative networks that are required to be interoperable if a trans-European network for the Interchange of Data between Administrations (TEN-IDA) is to be achieved. Initially, this requires that the existing constraints upon information flows need to be noted in areas such as the network architecture, bearer services and standardisation.

The evolution of the ENS fits into the development of other projects of common interest such as health care. The fact that many other schemes seek to use telematics to aid the provision of public services frequently means that communication and exchange of data between administrations is further necessitated. Generally, the ENS will be applied to a number of important sub-areas, notably environment, social services, emergency services and transport. The aim is to run these over a trans-European data service infrastructure which fits in with progress towards TEN-IBC.

The proposal for TEN-IDA[3] covers not only E-mail between administrations but also legal and architectural aspects, as well as assorted sectoral networks linked to the abolition of border controls. These include areas as diverse as fisheries, statistics, social security and medicinal products. It is proposed that TEN-IDA be established via a master plan guided by a multi-annual programme which oversees the development of projects of common interest over an initial three-year period. These actions are to be guided by the establishment of a high-level working group to co-ordinate actions both within and external to the EU.

Importantly, the development of TEN-IDA not only aims to initiate new administrative telematic applications, but also to integrate, under a common programme, existing initiatives taken by the Commission related to the administration of the European economic space. These initiatives include a scheme for data exchange for the imports and exports related to the customs union (CADDIA),[4] an inter-institutional information system (INSIS)[5] and electronic data interchange for trade (TEDIS).[6] Such integration under the umbrella of TEN-IDA should enable the exploitation of potential synergies between the assorted component programmes. As a consequence, these schemes have been re-prioritised, within the framework of TENs and other initiatives, as a response to the ongoing development of economic integration.

An immediate priority scheme within TEN-IDA has been the promotion of labour mobility by improving the exchange of data and other interlinkages between national social security offices and employment agencies. The monies devoted to the programme, some ECU180 million in the five years up to the year 2000, only represent a small proportion of the total needed for their development. Initial estimates suggest that the states will need to spend some ECU6 billion over five years of the project to ensure its attainment. An extra ECU7 billion over broadly the same period is required for peripheral areas that need greater adjustment in terms of computer and data transmission equipment (CEC 1995a). Once initial feasibility studies have been undertaken, funding may become available for the development of these networks in peripheral areas from more diverse sources such as the EIB.

A key theme in ensuring the marketability of the ENS is that the programmes engendered support user needs and the business imperatives of administrations. Each prioritised project, of which there are fourteen related to administrations within the telematics initiative,[7] has a development structure that reflects the broad user interests involved in its development. These have been complemented by the establishment of the Telematics in Administration Group (TAG) which seeks, via informal meetings of government and Commission officials, to ensure that developments within telematics are visible to relevant user communities in order to provide a means of ensuring the smooth infusion and diffusion of these applications into administrative structures. TAG is borne of a perceived common need to access these technologies, as well as addressing the concerns of interconnection and interoperability of the associated equipment.

The existing schemes have proved a mixed success; some have been widely adopted, while others are in danger of losing user support (Ridge 1994). If the applications fail, it is usually because scant attention has been given to user requirements in the initial stages of development. This situation can often be muddied if the end users are difficult to identify and if their requirements differ due to variations in economic development and technological sophistication.

The actual implementation of the procedure for TEN-IDA has hit a number of administrative hurdles. Despite being proposed in early 1993, it was not until mid-1996 that the final draft emerged. Part of the problem for the slow legislative process was that the Commission action was split into two separate decisions requiring distinct legislative procedures.[8]

Interoperability of administration networks in the EU is hindered by the nature of European communications which are often based upon heterogeneous applications and a multi-cultural/lingual environment. In other areas, the uneven development of infrastructure limits the application of telematics, as does the unwillingness to change old work habits. The interoperability required of the network necessitates connections between networks and VAN services as well as interconnection of application data. Many of the ENS issues have sought to solve interconnection/interoperability problems but to date this has only been a limited success. On the X.25 system, the major initial delivery system of the ENS, full interoperability has yet to be achieved. With the market for corporate data communications steadily evolving, the trend towards stable standards should be attained across a number of VAN suppliers. This should provide the basis for transparent interconnection and interoperability for the realisation of the ENS.

The successive phases of TEN-IDA have centred upon the desire to attain a critical mass for the commercial development of communications between administrations. The intention is that once this critical mass is achieved the uses of the technology can be extended further within the public administration sector and beyond. Such efforts will be aided by the development of the TESTA[9] scheme which aims to establish a common platform over which all types of services relevant to public administration can be offered. The interoperability and interconnection offered by TESTA could provide the means to ensure the success of TEN-IDA. Potentially TESTA offers the opportunity of lowering the costs of access to services. This should give greater incentives for both users and suppliers to sustain interest and investment in this series of telematic networks. As yet it is too soon to judge if this technology is to be the network driver envisaged by the Commission. Its successful development is likely to be pivotal in the overall credibility of the TEN-IDA policy with both users and suppliers.

Given the fact that administrative systems have taken centuries to reach their current form, it is unlikely that a common administrative framework will develop in the near future. Common telematic applications are likely to speed up the harmonisation of procedures though it is estimated that this will take some time (Baquiast 1993). Consequently, the development of a European Administrative Area is a distant reality. Despite the development of TAG, the lack of a strategic plan between administrations is delaying interconnection and interoperability, thereby hindering the full benefits of this technology (ibid.).[10] While the technology and the political will exist, there is still believed to be a reluctance to change old work habits within many organisations.

EVOLUTION OF TELEMATIC PROJECTS OF COMMON INTEREST

As already noted, the efforts of the EU are devoted to developing applications of socio-cultural and economic importance (including the ENS). These broad groups of projects possess a common theme of promoting the infusion and diffusion of a series of selected telematic applications throughout Europe's socio-economic strata. The choice of priority projects reflects market failure concerns and a broad desire to promote this technology as a complement to economic development and regeneration. Consequently, a key theme within many prioritised applications is to improve access by SMEs to telematic technology. The aim was to have 40 per cent of SMEs with access to telematic networks by the end of 1996.

Telematics is a recurrent theme throughout the EU's successive research initiatives (see Table 5.2). Such continuity and expansion is assisted by each successive scheme building on the results of the preceding programme. The range of applications prioritised and supported by the EU has expanded as its priorities have altered, most notably with the dilution of the emphasis upon SEM-linked applications towards those that stress growth and competitiveness. Aside from these evolving priorities, each of the successive research initiatives has stressed, as standard themes, the development of key common enabling technologies and systems, the cost-effective testing of applications within user environments and well-defined implementation strategies.

Interoperability and interconnection are set to be achieved within the assorted consortia, trans-national in nature, that make up the structure of the initiatives supported by the EU. These objectives are complemented by running such supranational funded schemes alongside relevant national projects as a means of exploiting synergies. Many telematic projects have developed as a result of partnerships between public–private sectors. Figure 5.1 indicates the sources of partners, across all geographic regions, for telematic programmes within the Third Framework initiative. In peripheral states, the involvement of SMEs was much greater, making nearly 40 per cent of all partners compared to 8 per cent for larger enterprises. This feature reflects SMEs as a dominant form of enterprise in peripheral regions.

Table 5.2 indicates the projects of common interest as defined by the EU over the successive framework programmes. These applications are relevant to socio-

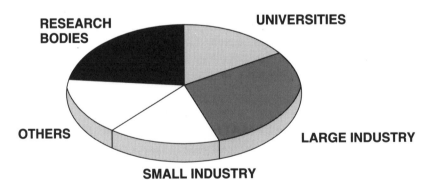

Figure 5.1 Sources of partners within Third Framework telematics programme
Source: Commission of the European Communities, 1993g

Table 5.2 Telematics within EU research policies

Second Framework Programme	Third Framework Programme	Fourth Framework Programme
• Healthcare (AIM) • Flexible and distance learning (DELTA) • Road transport (DRIVE)	• Exchange of data between administrations • Transport services • Healthcare • Flexible and distance learning • Rural areas • Libraries • Linguistic research and engineering	• Administrations • Transport • Research • Education and training • Libraries • Urban and rural areas • Healthcare • Disabled and elderly people • Environment • Assorted exploratory actions • Telematics engineering • Language engineering • Information engineering

Source: European Commission, various documents

cultural and public service environments. Despite being deemed of common interest, the ability of states to absorb these technologies within their respective socio-economic structures differs markedly. Their absorption within socio-economic structures will depend upon factors such as technological development of the economy and the quality of the infrastructure over which the information is carried. Despite the fact that many enterprises use some form of telematics, the ability of this technology to be absorbed into broader sectors that are not by nature information intensive is doubtful. Without a more mature information culture, it is unlikely that these technologies will fully deliver the anticipated economic benefits.

The initial concerns of the telematics scheme were to kick-start the development of projects that exhibit strong spillovers between member states. The initial priority schemes, reflected within the Second Framework, seemed to achieve little if any real tangible progress in the development of the technology. Part of the problem of drawing any conclusions are the differences that exist between the sectors concerned. For example, in the health sector there has been a larger quantity of funding for initial research as opposed to the pilots and demonstrations that have been undertaken in others. The schemes may have created a greater awareness of the role of telematics within services and economic development, but the full impact will only be felt and assessed over the medium to longer term. A frequent lack of strategic vision within programme development has led to disjointedness between projects. Many users still seem unconvinced of the relevance of telematics technology.[11] Access may be facilitated but the potential in terms of services and infrastructure is still not yet fully understood.

The EU provides a demonstration function by acting as a testbed for applications and offering commercial developers the opportunity and incentives to finance the selected applications. The aim is to test the value of these networks to the user and, over the longer term, to prove that their development as TENs is commercially and technologically feasible.

Over the short term, offering the prioritised applications over TEN-ISDN is a means of ensuring the end-to-end interoperability of telematic services, especially for those relevant to SMEs.[12] The aim is to offer these services over a common platform, enabling SMEs access to telematics throughout Europe. The use of TEN-ISDN, initially to deliver and set a framework for the development of this technology, reflects its immediacy and applicability to these services as well as its near universal roll-out by the end of the millennium. Thus initial action within TEN-Telecom is based upon consolidating ISDN as a delivery mechanism in readiness for the increased availability of broadband networks.

The Bangemann Report (Bangemann Group 1994) highlighted a series of priority applications, which despite similarities, reflected a more market-centred approach to telematic development. The Report pinpoints the importance of developing those applications linked to the attainment of critical mass which are by their nature more explicitly commercial than those prioritised by the Commission. This reflects a view that the market could deliver the Commission's prioritised socio-cultural applications once it has reached sufficient commercial maturity.

Despite such differences there are common themes in areas linked to public services and economic development such as healthcare, traffic management, distance learning, research, air traffic control, SMEs, teleworking and public administrations. These exist alongside applications that are more deliberately designed for explicitly commercial ends, notably city information highways used to deliver entertainment services. Each of these priority applications has been set non-binding targets which are indicators of the degree of progression made by the EU towards the information society.

How active the public sector needs to be in the development of these applications depends on user responsiveness. As a result many of them are and will be tested within information intensive environments to test their marketability. Though the Commission does not exclude such explicitly commercial applications, it believes they do not require prioritisation. It perceives as more important the realisation of those services/applications which are socially and economically useful that the market may otherwise fail to deliver.

THE TELEMATICS INITIATIVE (1994–8)

Building on the results of previous framework programmes, the Fourth Framework has set about developing telematic networks across the EU in a more coherent and holistic manner. Aside from the development of the ENS, the Commission has identified seven key areas to be promoted in the domain of telematics:

1 Transport: assorted initiatives such as DRIVE have sought to utilise this technology to relieve concerns caused by congestion and poor inter-modal management.

2 Researchers: to interlink universities to facilitate the dissemination of knowledge with the eventual aim of this spilling over into commercial applications.

3 Education/training and libraries: this seeks to improves access to training schemes and education by enterprises of all sizes, irrespective of their location. In terms of libraries, the aim is to interconnect assorted important sites to render these a common resource.

4 Urban and rural: this involves the promotion of activities such as teleworking which perceptibly promote the economic development of rural areas and inner cities. The application of this technology is seen as a precursor for renewed investment in these areas.

5 Healthcare and elderly/disabled care: existing schemes such as AIM have a legacy of investment in telematics for the health sector in terms of the elderly and disabled. The aim is to use the technology to reduce the need for mobility, e.g. smart houses.

6 Environment and other exploratory actions: an examination of what telematics could do to promote sustainable development. There is also a commitment by the EU to explore the possibility of extending this action to any other sector where it is believed that the technology could be of relevance.

7 Language, telematics and information engineering: these aim to promote the technology within a multilingual environment by utilising the information in its most user-friendly format.

Within the context of the Fourth Framework, the emphasis of policy has been upon the development of 'infostructure' in three key areas: public interest; knowledge; quality of life. The allocation of resources within the programme is shown in Figure 5.2. The user-led approach to the development of projects is seen as important, not only for reasons of successful marketability and the transformation of specific applications into generic services, but also as a means of identifying existing fragmentation.

While initial emphasis is focused upon proving the marketability of the technology, effort is also being centred upon preparing the groundwork for the future development of more innovative services. Thus the development of this technology, as a means of supporting the shift to the information society, is evolutionary. As the potential of telematics expands, the Commission hopes that this will be reflected in better applications of the technology throughout the socio-economic structure. Ultimately such shifts will be user pulled not technology pushed.

The broader themes stressed within the Fourth Framework Programme indicate how the Commission believes the technology has the potential to influence many areas of the economy. An open-ended commitment to explore the development of telematic solutions in other areas, as yet unspecified, underlines such

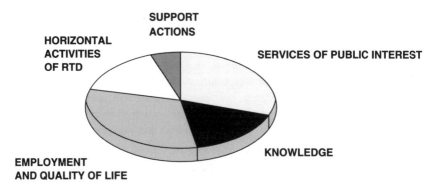

Figure 5.2 Telematics application programme, division of support under Fourth Framework

Source: European Commission

a belief. Chosen applications are designed directly to support the Commission's strategy of aiding economic regeneration and renewal in a cohesive manner. Typical to other research initiatives, the development of telematics is promoted within forums that reflect the mutuality of interest involved in this technology.

The aim of the initiatives is to extend the life of existing infrastructure and to plot more readily the shift towards broadband. Another key feature is the prominence given to users and affordability in the development process. While this has always been important, it has never been stressed as heavily before and perhaps reflects the newly liberalised telecommunications environment within which the project partners are now operating. The desire of the EU is specifically to promote those schemes that would gather support from enterprises which would eventually offer them commercially. In terms of the life cycle of projects, this is reflected in that fact that the Commission aims to devote 50 per cent of resources to ensuring the validation of these projects with users in real-life situations. This represents what is perhaps the key theme, that telematics must be seen to be doing something for users. In practice this is the foundation stone of the market-led development of telematic networks. The telematics scheme is designed to take place within the context of the other Fourth Framework initiatives, Esprit and ACTS, each of which is designed to complement the development of the information society within user-led strategies.

Table 5.3 Funding for telematics from Fourth Framework Programme

Proposals received	Funding requested (million ECU)	Proposals selected	Funding recommended (million ECU)
1375	4373	290	424

Source: Rapid Reports, 'Green Light for First Projects in the New ACTs, Esprit and Telematic Applications Programmes' (IP/95/850)

104

TELEMATICS AND REGIONAL DEVELOPMENT

Telematics are perceived by the Commission as having a generally positive influence upon regional development. Their importance has perceptibly increased as the EU has expanded and divergences, a natural consequence of this expansion, have grown wider. The active promotion of telematics in peripheral areas seeks to address the following ambitions:

- to create conditions for more dispersed SMEs to provide employment and a more balanced economic structure;
- to establish the basis for improved public services;
- to increase the level of awareness of the role of ICTs;
- to encourage equipment and service suppliers to make equipment more easily accessible to rural areas;
- to promote harmonised planning in terms of advanced communications infrastructures in rural areas;
- to ensure that improved network provision in rural areas does not result in further centralisation.

Differences in technological development are likely to be reinforced as a consequence of the relative rapidity of the core region in pushing towards the information society. Specific action for telematic services related to regional development were introduced within the Third Framework Programme. Within the Fourth Framework Programme, urban and rural perspectives are again prioritised. In practice this means the utilisation of generic services and applications (such as teleworking) to these environments as a method of promoting their development. In addition to these research initiatives, the growth of these networks has been aided by structural funding under the STAR and Télématique initiatives.

Since the digitalisation of peripheral networks advanced by STAR, the emphasis has switched to demand stimulation via the widespread promotion of telematic applications and services. This reinforces a key issue of space not being a retardant to the consumption of the prioritised public interest services. Despite this stance, the positioning of the EU is that the development of telematic networks takes priority over concerns of regional development. Only when the technology is developed will methods actively be sought to apply telematics to the concerns of cohesion.

Despite regional development being a lay concern in the current framework, many regions have decided to collaborate to ensure that they are not left behind by such advancements. Some have come together to establish a European Community Teleworking Forum to support the advent of this form of telematics services as a direct complement to the growth process. The forum acts to promote the development of relevant applications, via advice on areas such as consortia formation and disseminating R&D results. Other initiatives include RITE[13] which seeks to provide SMEs in the periphery with access to the Internet.

While keen to push generic applications such as teleworking and E-mail, only a very small proportion of STAR funding (some 15 per cent) went on demand and supply stimulation. There seemed to be little point in stimulating the demand for services which infrastructure could not deliver. While STAR provided some funding for the development of advanced services, its primary focus was upon developing the infrastructure. Figure 5.3 reflects the anticipated manner in which STAR was to promote regional development. The infrastructure focus of STAR was in part superseded by the applications, services and access approach followed by its successor, Télématique. The Télématique scheme sought to derive increased economic value from the infrastructure developed by STAR through the employment of assorted telematic applications relevant to SME development in these regions. Télématique was seen by many as a success not only in terms of increasing the quality of services available but also in making a contribution to improvements in the quality of life within these areas.[14] Some states disliked such an emphasis, believing that a greater focus upon improving human capital could make a more effective contribution to the economic development of these regions. Private-led development of these networks has been hindered by the lack of technological development in these areas and the relatively poor density of telecommunication lines and users.

These regional schemes are not R&D programmes but reflect concerns of deployment (see later). They are about improving access to existing technology by peripheral regions though closer interaction between regional and research policies is evident. While these schemes focus on both sides of the market, the demand side, as reflected in the telematics and telecom-TENs initiatives, has become a more prominent area of policy. Traditionally, policy has centred upon the supply-side requirements and ignored the fact that poor demand was, and remains, the biggest retardant to the full penetration of these services in peripheral areas. Such a limitation is likely to do little to reverse its relatively poor level of technological development. This limited demand will exhibit itself in underinvestment right throughout the network.

The marketability of telematic services to these regions without enhanced state or EU support is extremely doubtful. These areas suffer not only from inadequate infrastructure provision but also the poor availability of trained human resources, a retarded business sector and a production system geared towards local markets. Often the differing priorities within states mean that it is difficult to synthesise policy measures. Differing business structures and state objectives can and will sway investment.

These telecommunications initiatives (STAR and Télématique) have had a generally positive impact upon regional development by adding velocity to national investments in telecommunications infrastructure (Ewbank Preece 1993). They have improved the telecommunications situation of most of the states, although investment in Greece has actually tended to decline over the period during which these projects were active. Perhaps the greatest effects will be felt over the longer term as awareness grows of the potential of

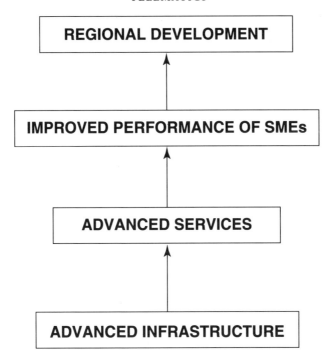

Figure 5.3 How the EU's regional telecom schemes were meant to work
Source: *I&T News Review*, 1994, autumn, p.2

telecommunications in regional development. These schemes have tended to be criticised for lacking interlinkages and not exploiting synergies between particular projects. Ewbank Preece (ibid.) feels that its effects have been limited by the concentration upon value added services which were generally of more use to large enterprises than to SMEs. Many SMEs simply did not have the technological sophistication and such awareness was not directly funded through these schemes. The lessons from these schemes for policy-makers are to push for the development of services that genuinely assist growth and technological development.

The impact of telematics in terms of converging economic development is debatable. Clearly infrastructure provision is only half the issue; it is only as good as the applications and services provided over it. Such applications and services determine the value to users. If the core regions tend to be more sophisticated in terms of telecommunications and computing they will utilise the technology more effectively and enhance their economic advantages relative to the periphery. Therefore the core is able to exploit the potentialities afforded by telematics and new emerging forms of division of labour to its own advantage. Thus telematics may promote agglomeration, not dispersion as many anticipate. This underlines the importance for peripheral areas to engage in the promotion of ICT skills within their labour markets and to develop an awareness of telematics within SMEs.

NATIONAL AND GLOBAL DIMENSIONS OF EUROPE'S TELEMATICS INITIATIVES

The development of telematic networks associated with these schemes is increasingly within the context of action taken at national and global levels. This hierarchy of growth reflects the increasing international interdependencies of national networks.

To date many national initiatives have focused upon the commercial aspects of the deployment and development of telematic networks. For corporate networking, telematics have been widely used for some time. A noticeable trend, and one which is important in realising a priority of the EU, is that the consumption of telematic services is becoming increasingly important for SMEs as well as large commercial concerns. The development of projects on a national level that directly parallels those prioritised by the EU has only resulted in limited progress towards their realisation. There have been limited trials and a number of telematic islands have been established. However, the commercial priorities of the PTOs, which are the major developers of these projects, have limited their enthusiasm. As a consequence many PTOs seek to propagate such projects within the framework of TENs.

Action by states is perceived as a necessary complement to those taken by the EU given the levels of funding required to develop the prioritised applications. A common theme between EU action and the initiatives promoted by many European states is in increasing the potential of the existing infrastructure as a means of supplying advanced services to more diverse user communities. Such synergies offer the potential for achieving interoperability and interconnection between assorted national and supranational schemes at the development stage. Often the EU may make funding to aid national initiatives contingent upon these prerequisites being in place, reinforcing the links and spillovers between national and Community-wide initiatives.

Alongside these national schemes are others of a transnational nature such as IRSIS.[15] This scheme aims to establish the infrastructure to deliver the EU's priority applications to participating regions. Again any support given by the EU is on the precondition that it evolves in an interoperable and interconnected manner with other schemes being developed elsewhere.

Many of the applications developed as part of the EU telematics programme are also of direct relevance to broader global trends. Within the G7 forum, states have started to collaborate and share results when developing telematic networks of mutual interest. This mutuality of interest is born of the desire of all of these states to retain their relative economic position as globalisation has a greater perceptible impact upon their economies. Collaboration seeks to utilise the more advanced technological and telecommunication systems of these states to sustain their competitive edge over emerging competitors. The G7 has developed a number of telematic pilot projects which are designed to exploit the synergies of existing schemes.

In Brussels, in early 1995, the G7 states highlighted a series of pilot projects designed to address issues of common concern in a number of key areas, notably related to the individual (such as health or libraries), to the economy (in areas such as SMEs and broadband networks) and to broad public concerns (such as global emergencies or the environment). These actions are to be complemented by the establishment of a global inventory of applications and studies which seeks to develop or create the conditions within which transnational alliances can be established as a precursor of developing priority applications.

Such developments are integral to the emergence of the global information infrastructure and the freer flow of information across borders which is its immediate prerequisite. The advancement of these applications, combined with the successful realisation of freer trade in telecommunication services, offers the potential benefit of increased investment in network infrastructure globally by the public and private sectors. While not limited to Europe, such developments offer opportunities for European enterprises to exploit their advantages in the promotion, delivery and utilisation of the global information infrastructure. Inevitably such global interoperability and interconnection is likely to be hindered by the failure of the respective partners to agree on the ability of operators to move information freely across borders without some form of regulatory restriction.

DEPLOYMENT OF TELEMATICS

Where technologies are being deployed throughout the EU this occurs in response to commercial pressures. To date telematics technology is being used within enterprise networks of all sizes. The importance of this process to the EU's priorities is the gradual deployment and targeting by operators of the SME sector. However, the interest of commercial operators in other priority sectors seems to be minimal. As a consequence the EU is undertaking an active deployment strategy to push the infusion of the priority projects throughout Europe's socio-economic structure. These are taking place within the telecom-TENs initiative.

Deployment is an increasingly important theme and is complementary to research ventures. Such deployment measures are concerted efforts by public bodies to stimulate the demand for these technologies via the prioritised services and applications.[16] These efforts need to be complemented further by actions to improve supply-side related aspects of deployment, most notably labour skills and economies of scale in equipment manufacturing.

The objective is to push the utilisation of telematics, as part of the promotion of TEN-ISDN, up to the point where the development of prioritised applications attracts private funding and is able to divorce itself from public sector support. In short, policy offers support up to where the market has sufficient incentive to take over deployment. These applications are in part intended to ensure the mass consumption of advanced services. The aim is to utilise the technology to produce specific and generic applications that could drive the market for information services and create a culture that is more open to the desired technological developments.

The deployment and development of the prioritised networks is envisaged to take place within public and private partnerships (PPPs). These are promoted to develop applications that are of uncertain commercial feasibility. The Commission's thinking is to stimulate socio-applications using private sector expertise and finance which is partially subsidised by the public sector. PPPs, in this context, are direct market creating devices. Their existence in deployment strategies is an implicit recognition that, if left to its own devices, the commercial sector would have little incentive to provide services which were largely untested and of doubtful commercial feasibility. PPPs are therefore designed to overcome such technological and commercial inertia.

The deployment of telematics is complemented by action at the national level. The UK's market-led Information Society Initiative seeks to provide access to telematics by SMEs, primarily by promoting an enhanced awareness of the potential role of ICTs within these enterprises. The initiative is essentially a public–private partnership to stimulate a mature market for ICTs. A priority within the initiative is to ensure compatibility with supranational initiatives, thereby enabling extra funding to become available from these sources. This initiative is promoted as a direct complement to the development of telecom-TENs. Other states also have parallel initiatives, for example the German Info 2000 scheme. While both of these pursue a demand stimulation approach to network deployment, they each recognise the importance of complementary supply-side measures to the process.

The deployment strategy followed by the EU does have its problems. The fascination with socio-cultural applications and those relevant to SMEs runs the risk of encountering a number of problems. First, the major customers for socio-cultural applications would be public service providers, very often the state. This is a sector that is currently undergoing substantial expenditure cuts. Consequently their ability to deploy this technology may be limited. A second problem is that there is a real danger of technology developing ahead of the requirements of the user. Thus schemes may be promoted that have little relevance for current or potential user requirements. Once users are brought more closely into the process of network development the specific relevance of telematics will become more evident. A third issue is how sensitive and flexible is the labour force to the requirements of increased telematic usage.

Interrelated are the financing gaps which are emerging for the applications prioritised by the EU. This indicates that the private sector is not investing in these applications in the quantity desired. Such gaps may emerge due to the uncertainty of demand for the technology, the ability and willingness of the end user to purchase the services in the desired quantity, a simple lack of interest, or that the public sector is not putting enough resources into the partnerships – thereby expecting the private sector to bear a greater degree of risk than it is prepared to shoulder.

In the development of TENs, the demand for these applications is seen as the ultimate driver behind the development of investment in infrastructure. Indeed, within the telecom-TENs deployment strategy, the Commission is hoping that such applications will drive the wider roll-out of TEN-ISDN as a precursor for the development of TEN-IBC. Deployment has been a poor second best to the research effort upon telematic networks. Speculatively, if more resources were ploughed into deployment the upturn in demand may stimulate the desired advancement in research. The market is probably the best decider of what is needed and the applications prioritised by the EU will be provided by such forces if the demand is there. As users become entwined within the telecom-TENs initiative, their preferences will increasingly determine its success. Only if the needs of users match the desires of the EU will the prioritised telematic networks develop.

CONCLUSION

Telematic networks, as prioritised by the EU, are about delivering socio-economic functionality. The market has proved itself capable of producing a broad range of telematic networks and applications to the business sector. Already it is apparent that the market is unlikely to be a satisfactory medium for the delivery of the prioritised applications and services. The level of technological sophistication and demand for these networks is still at a level below the critical mass desired for market delivery. Direct policy measures, in terms of funding for projects, is likely to prove ineffectual for the realisation of these networks.

Probably more effective will be policies to stimulate the demand for these networks via the series of measures to increase awareness among users of telematics technology. By aiding and promoting access to this technology by more diverse user groups, the public sector hopes to attain the critical mass needed for commercial delivery. It is as yet unclear as to whether such measures will be a success. These schemes are still at an embryonic phase and it is still not possible to judge their success in achieving the desired aim.

The development of these networks is hindered by the uneven growth of delivery channels. In other ways the practical delivery of information is also impeded by the practicalities of communication within a multilingual/multi-cultural environment. These issues are compounded by concerns such as those related to the security of the information transmitted over the network.

The results of the EU funded PEPITA[17] project have highlighted that actors within key sectors such as healthcare, education, administration, assorted public and commercial bodies, have indicated that many recognise the benefits from telematics in terms of better services and improved access to and exchange of information. However, these are countered by assorted hesitancies derived from a culture that does not readily accept this technology, from ineffective standards, poor training, lack of affordability and poor infrastructure. In addition it was felt that many SMEs did not possess the degree of technological sophistication required to offer a lucrative market to commercial operators. This is important, for the key sectors involved in realising the EU's priorities have mixed feelings about this technology. Such technological inertia will inevitably hinder the broader usage of telematic networks.

6

TRANS-EUROPEAN INTEGRATED BROADBAND TELECOMMUNICATION NETWORKS (TEN-IBC)

INTRODUCTION

ISDN as a TEN is based upon utilising existing technology to ensure the delivery of more advanced services over what is essentially a narrowband network. The longer term objective of many states is more clearly focused upon the widespread provision of the 'information superhighway'. To many this highway is represented by the delivery of advanced multi-media services over an Integrated Broadband Communications (IBC) infrastructure. The 'integrated' aspect of IBC is a reference not only to the integration of services highlighted within ISDN but also to the interoperability and interconnection of a conglomeration of networks.

The development of IBC is not the end point of network evolution, but is an important staging post in the economic opportunities perceived to be available from advanced telecommunications. While offering the greatest potential it also represents the greatest economic and logistical challenge. The development of this network implies a series of important challenges from the wholescale renewal of the entire infrastructure through to the relevant services, applications and technology.

The ultimate theme of this chapter is to plot the migration strategies of suppliers and policy-makers towards this advanced form of networking. Commercial forces and private actors will be pivotal in IBC development with the public sector tending to perform a role that complements, facilitates and creates market processes.[1] After focusing upon the main features of integrated broadband communications networks this chapter goes on to examine the major initiatives, both policy induced and commercially led, to develop the network of networks that will comprise TEN-IBC. Thereafter the technology is examined in relation to the marketability of broadband services. The chapter concludes by setting the network within the context of regional development and global interoperability.

FORM AND NATURE OF TEN-IBC

Broadband networking is based upon the utilisation of a network capacity of 2Mbp/s and above.[2] The importance of this broad bandwidth lay in the wider variety of services and applications which can be offered, actually and potentially, be over an integrated network. Many of the advanced services and applications designed to support the development of the information society require significant bandwidth if they are to be delivered successfully to the end user. TEN-IBC is not a single, holistic concept for it is based upon a network of networks. Thus TEN-IBC is a virtual network whose existence depends on mutually agreed interoperability and interconnection decisions.

Despite being available since the mid-1970s (for broadcasting services), broadband technology has only recently started to become ingrained within national telecommunication networks. While all EU PTOs have fibre optic broadband backbones, the key economic and political challenge (as will be noted later) is in infusing IBC deep within Europe's socio-economic strata to an extent that it delivers tangible benefits throughout the economy. This desire is reflected in the fact that SMEs and the labour market have been identified and prioritised as key action areas for IBC development and deployment. To achieve the full competitive effects from the network, the market for this technology has to reach a critical mass that enables it to realise a density equivalent to the prevailing copper-based analogue network. Indeed TEN-IBC has sought to use, where possible, existing infrastructure technology as a means of access to fibre optic broadband networks.

Visions of the potential of broadband networking often tend to avoid commercial realities. In many cases enterprises are simply not ready and do not require the extra functionality offered by advanced networks. Such uncertainty strains the market-led strategy for the roll-out of the IBC network. Limits to technological advancements of users have held back consumption of advanced services and, according to the European Parliament, have led to a growing difference in information and communication usage between the EU and its major competitors; this factor has reduced Europe's commercial success over the last decade or so.

The convergence of IT and telecommunications and interaction with other sectors, notably broadcasting, are leading to the development of multi-media services. Multi-media highlight the fuller evolution of telecommunications as their traditional aural basis is complemented by services and applications that utilise wider sensory perceptions. Such trends are noticeable by the wider range of operators from the traditional PTOs through to software companies, publishers and broadcasters which are becoming involved in advanced network development.[3] The flexibility within the network should enable the user to demand the services desired rather than simply to accept what the PTO is prepared to supply. Such developments are in part a response to the increased intensity of competition within the sector.

The impetus behind the development of broadband networking has come from governments and other regulatory bodies that have sought to create the opportunities for network growth and deployment by addressing market failure issues and promoting IBC within the various sectors involved in its evolution. Its progress has also been aided by the establishment of industry bodies such as the ATM forum which seeks to accelerate the spread of broadband products and services through the rapid establishment of interoperability specifications and promotion of broad industrial co-operation. Public and private interests in broadband reflect a diversity of concerns, though common ground exists in ensuring pre-competitive interoperability and interconnection as precursors to achieving their respective ambitions.

DEVELOPING A STRATEGY FOR MIGRATION TO TEN-IBC

The major drivers behind the shift towards broadband networking techniques are the larger, often multinational, enterprises that are more sensitive to technological change and its effects upon performance. The increased sophistication and geographical diversity of corporate communications, in combination with a generally liberal regulatory regime, have focused the attention of larger, often PTO-based, carriers on delivering business solutions at higher bandwidth. This has been the most evident form of broadband networking within local and wide area networks.[4] The experience of the USA has highlighted the importance of business services and applications in attaining the desired level of critical mass for broadband networks. Many users go for broadband as a means of obtaining a large quantity of bandwidth on demand which enables them to achieve greater efficiency and functionality from corporate communications.

The strategy of broadening the use of IBC to all forms and sizes of enterprise reflects the Commission's position that the network will not assist industrial competitiveness if it is limited to narrowly defined niche markets. The EU strategy seeks to stimulate the market for broadband technology to meet these objectives. Commercial dynamism rather than state direction is increasingly determining levels of deployment. Any public sector strategy is based upon manipulating these forces to meet broader social, cultural and economic objectives.

Consequently the major focus of TEN-IBC strategy is to address issues of market failure. Its status within the EU's industrial policy is as a network that will evolve with and support the transformation of user requirements. For a sustained period into the next millennium TEN-IBC is likely to progress alongside ISDN. This reflects the desire that IBC should not overshadow the potential economic benefits from ISDN which offers more short-term competitive and industrial policy solutions. The differences between the capabilities of ISDN, the limits of markets and the desires of industrial policy have provoked policy action in the public sector at national and supranational level to develop IBC as a TEN.

The migration from ISDN to IBC is compounded by a number of issues (Stehmann 1995). The impact of these detrimental factors depends upon the strategy chosen and the relative salience of competition in networking versus the desirability of developing advanced networks. First, the development of a universal IBC network potentially raises barriers to entry which could be used as a justification for state control or intervention. Second, in the switch to IBC from ISDN, there is a trade-off between fixed and marginal cost. In terms of IBC, the former will rise and the latter will fall. This again makes competition within the sector more difficult. Third, the excess capacity delivered by the network can also be used as a deterrent against entry. Such scenarios arise from a pattern of migration based upon allowing the incumbent to sustain its dominant position. These features are compounded due to high sunk costs which add further friction to the migration process. Stehmann (1995) argues that this top-down approach is inferior to one that seeks to develop and promote the migration of ISDN to IBC via a more federative system of networking.

The decision to prioritise IBC is a controversial one.[5] The EU is effectively trying to determine not only what is sent over the network, in terms of applications and services, but is also attempting, according to some PTOs, to dictate its form of delivery. Such complaints have to be seen as rather hollow for the wishes of the EU cannot translate in practice due to its relatively poor funding position. The EU's perspective is inherently long term whereas PTOs are facing more short-term challenges. Commercial rather than socio-economic concerns will drive investment into IBC.

INDUSTRIAL POLICY INITIATIVES AT EUROPEAN LEVEL

There are two aspects to the European Commission's strategy for the development of broadband networks: the first is a series of research and development initiatives; the second is a network deployment policy. These are complemented to varying degrees by other EU-supported initiatives such as Esprit (information technology), Eureka (backbone infrastructure)[6] and IMPACT (developing a common information market). The collaborative nature of the broadband research programmes reflects, from the experience of previous research initiatives, the perceived positive impact of these structures upon enterprises (Dodgson 1993). Thus, as an EU policy area TEN-IBC is best understood as a means of co-ordinating actions of operators to achieve the desired outcomes.

The anticipated changes promoted by the development of the broadband network and the mutuality of interest in its evolution have facilitated co-operation and collaboration at national, supranational and international levels. Each of these developments tends to contribute towards the broader common objectives of transnational interconnection and interoperability – key aims of TEN-IBC. Such collaborations can also provide information about the networking environment. The greater the information about technological preferences and progress the easier it is likely to be for the network to develop as required. Therefore schemes not only play a part in technological development but also perform a signalling role to parties inside and outside the sector. Collaborative research schemes, especially those on a transnational level, are important in creating a convergent set of attitudes in network development and promoting common interests such as SME access to broadband. Despite such co-operation, divergences remain between states in their sensitivity to developments within the information market.

Research into broadband networking holds many potential gains for European enterprises which policy seeks to harness.[7] The development of the network has potential implications for the competitive positioning of most if not all enterprises. A further initial aim is that the indigenous enterprises from the sectors involved in the development of TEN-IBC (broadly speaking telecommunications, IT and broadcasting) use Europe's move to advanced networks to attain a globally competitive position within their respective areas.

In the conceptual stage of IBC in 1984 three phases were distinguished. The first concentrated upon the system engineering, specifications and key technologies. The second focused upon the integration and prototyping of new services and applications. The third was based upon user orientated experiments. These phases found their concerns reflected in RACE I, RACE II and ACTS correspondingly. Phase three would have to differ markedly from the previous

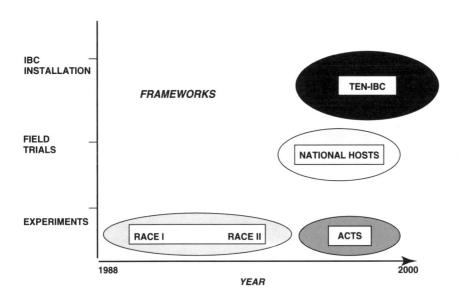

Figure 6.1 Phasing of IBC implementation
Source: European Commission

117

two in terms of management and structure; thus there is a separate programme and not simply RACE III. As suggested in Figure 6.1 the above complementary schemes seek the advancement of the network to the end of the millennium. ACTS (see below) aims to shift IBC out of the laboratories into open trials and eventual widespread installation.

Research into Advanced Communications in Europe (RACE)

The RACE programme comprised two distinct phases: RACE I running from 1988 through to 1992; RACE II from 1991 to 1994. RACE II was less of a theoretical expression of IBC than RACE I and sought to push for the integration of services and applications over a single virtual network rather than developing the technology. The overarching aim of RACE was to establish a competitive and strategic European presence in development of IBC networks. There are three main aspects to RACE: first, consensus formation and development and implementation strategies; second, the technologies; third, the application pilots and verification.

The migration strategy implied within the RACE initiative involves the expansion of the assorted European fibre optic networks in a manner conducive to the objectives of TENs. Initial action sought interconnection and interoperability by the development of common functional specifications (within transnational research consortia) for the introduction of services utilising broadband technology. This was to be the basis for the development of a backbone telecommunications network by the mid-1990s (see below).

RACE only partially alleviated the fragmentation and uneven development of Europe's telecommunications environment. Such phenomena will only be overcome by research policies that act in concert with other relevant policies such as those devoted to the promotion of competition within the sector. RACE, in retrospect, was the initial stage in network development. The major successes were derived from its ability to set the agenda for the evolution of IBC, as well as adding impetus. As the importance of the network broadens, so the scheme is likely to be seen as a landmark on the road to IBC in Europe. The programme could only ever be partially successful in the development of IBC due to the time frame over which it was operating.

Compared to previous research initiatives, project development in RACE was more pluralistic, with a wider range of interests represented. Such diversity of interests reflected the regulatory and technological changes which the sector was undergoing throughout the duration of the RACE initiatives. Increased user involvement reflected the importance of demand pull factors in network deployment and development and was perceived as a necessary prerequisite to the broader adoption of this technology within a wider range of user groups. Though RACE did not involve an explicit strategy to move from ISDN to IBC, it was important in setting the preconditions for the form of this migration.

RACE had a narrower focus than many preceding R&D schemes; some believe this enhanced its effectiveness.[8] The scheme brought together European specialists in the field of broadband communications and was able to make some concrete results in areas such as developing harmonious switching methods for broadband and agreements on the technology (ATM) to support network development. The consensus established within RACE about the way the network will develop has been seen to make a valuable contribution to furthering IBC evolution. Inevitably a common position on the form and nature of broadband should assist its harmonious roll-out within the EU.

The expectations and significance of the work involved in RACE became more prominent as the economic importance of telecommunications and its environment changed over the lifetime of the programme. RACE was overtaken by events such as the rise of multi-media. Many criticised RACE for its desire to build IBC based upon ISDN believing such a strategy would retard deployment.[9] The investments made by PTOs in ISDN give them a direct incentive to use such a strategy to slow the deployment of IBC. Changes in the regulatory environment have placed increased emphasis upon network renewal. The development of IBC via ISDN may be rational, given the uncertainty of demand for services of the preceding technology. If the demand for ISDN is non-existent then it would be difficult to justify investment in ever more advanced technology throughout the network.

How history will judge RACE's contribution to the technological development of Europe is still too soon to tell. Looking at the scheme in hindsight, the programme may seem relatively unambitious given the challenges we now know are posed by the development of the information economy. The legacy of RACE remains in schemes such as ACTS and in the evolution of transnational broadband projects. Despite this many believe that changes in the nature of telecommunications research and market liberalisation are making collaborative ventures such as RACE increasingly anachronistic.[10]

Preparatory actions for TEN-IBC[11]

As a continuation of the RACE programme, which ended in 1994, the European Commission put forward a series of actions to develop more fully the migration to TEN-IBC. Initially action focused on a common set of specifications to enable the trials of several key applications such as citizen networks, R&D networks, industry networks, business networks, administrative networks and media networks.

The key theme of these preparatory actions is to establish a learning curve for the development of applications and services linked to the deployment of TEN-IBC and identify what the network should deliver to strengthen industrial competitiveness. Such concerns will be realised over networks developed at both national and supranational level. To maintain interoperability and interconnection, these national initiatives are set within a broader transnational framework where there is general agreement between relevant bodies upon the form and type of services to be delivered.

Generally the intention of this set of actions, namely to define TEN-IBC and test its marketability, has been broadly achieved. Its initial emphasis upon the application of IBC to manufacturing as a means of strengthening its competitiveness[12] has been extended to specific niche markets within the service sector. This reflects a trend of promoting the migration towards TEN-IBC by developing and applying the technology to meet the needs and requirements of highly specified user groups.

Any problems associated with this action frequently stemmed from the fact that these projects utilised Asynchronous Transfer Mode (ATM) for their transmission. Difficulties in developing international ATM links and incompatibilities in ATM routes, factors outside the projects' control, tended to hinder the initial success. Taking a longer-term perspective the successful development of these projects and the migration of their more generic use into other groups are closely tied to the development of ATM technology. The development of generic usage is an issue that is increasingly at the heart of Europe's strategy for migrating to broadband (see below).

Advanced Communications Technologies and Services (ACTS)

The primary objective of ACTS, the successor programme to RACE, is to develop advanced communication systems and services utilising the IBC technology developed within the previous programmes (see Figure 6.1). ACTS is essentially about turning RACE into reality, shifting from research into trials and demonstrations. It seeks to find a practical use for the technology rather than putting further resources into its research and development with a key emphasis upon multi-media and high-speed networking.

ACTS covers the period from 1994 to 1998 with the EU committing ECU630 million for many cost-sharing contracts. Like previous initiatives it seeks to establish co-operative agreements between all parts of the sector, including non-European enterprises. This reflects a priority that the ACTS scheme should combine with those being developed in Japan and the USA and ensures that its results are disseminated to the emerging economies of central and Eastern Europe. The diversity of concerns reflected in broadband is reflected within the number of sources for partners involved in project development (see Table 6.1).

The starting-point for the development of the scheme is the advancement of ATM as established under the RACE initiative. The work is set to evolve in three stages: first, the identification of user needs; second, the integration of existing networks by developing missing links; third, the development of a series of interconnected networks to provide a test bed for the services prioritised.

Much of the work for the development of projects linked to ACTs will be performed upon 'national host' infrastructures with trials focused upon niche user groups. The eventual aim is to use trials upon the national hosts to promote interconnection and interoperability of the dispersed networks as precursors to their full integration. The use of national hosts as part of the programme is designed to improve access to the services by targeted user groups. Such national hosts include telecommunication operators, both public and private, and assorted broadcasting organisations. This highlights a shift away from a totally integrated and uniform solution for European telecommunications and uses national co-operation in its place. States will continue to work together on some programmes such as SONAH.[13]

A feature of ACTS is that it will not offer funding for infrastructure. Funding is only available for those applications that utilise existing infrastructure or for the national hosts. The use of funding to develop broadband infrastructure in remote areas has ceased. In short a multi-speed technological Europe has been officially sanctioned. This reflects the desire that peripheral areas should not hold back others; better that the technology develops somewhere in Europe rather than nowhere or elsewhere is the attitude of policy-makers. If commerce is to dictate the migration then factors such as user density will be relevant. This reflects a failure of RACE where projects funded in peripheral areas were often commercially unsustainable after the scheme finished. The network needs to be viewed holistically; therefore infrastructure cannot be viewed in isolation as it was in RACE.

Such a perspective highlights the view from the EU that the fundamental objective of ACTS has to be the network. Commercial services such as tele-shopping or video-on-demand exist but they are useless without the network. This is essential for their successful deployment throughout Europe's socio-economic strata. The development of standards to interconnect Europe and the broadband islands has been a central feature. The rise of the Internet and access technology are providing the standards for applications.[14] Some feel that these standards will create a single telecommunications market rather than those developed by the EU. In short the market may increasingly dictate the form of broadband network that evolves in Europe.

Table 6.1 Participation in ACTS

Key actors	Percentage of ACTS projects involved #
Industrial systems developers	60
Network operators	40
Broadcasters and service content providers	negligible
Key research organisations*	65
Non-EU bodies	9
Small and medium-sized enterprises	29

Source: European Commission
Notes:
This figure is based upon the source of proposals submitted.
* Includes major research laboratories.

The standards issue aside, Europe is already envisaging what to do beyond ACTS. One of the key items, which is a research theme within ACTS, is the development of photonic networks. The aim is to utilise fully the bandwidth available and increase exponentially the array of services obtainable. The document *ACTS 2000 Plus*[15] highlighted concerns of information overload derived from the sheer quantity available from the network. Research may need to focus upon relevance and ensure that information can be handled for optimal economic effect.

EU deployment strategies

The EU R&D initiatives foresee the deployment of TEN-IBC from the mid-1990s with an indicative implementation schedule as highlighted in Table 6.2. The schedule has tended to lag due to the sluggish roll-out of ISDN. As a consequence the Commission has developed a more coherent deployment strategy. Over the period 1997–9 it is seeking to push the deployment of ISDN, exploiting its synergies with IBC, and speed the penetration of advanced services throughout Europe's socio-economic structures.

Essentially, the EU's deployment strategies work on both the demand and supply side of the emerging market for broadband networks. Initially action towards this objective is based upon enhancing existing themes to establish and interconnect a number of broadband islands produced under industrial policy initiatives such as RACE. The development of IBC islands has as its modern translation the development of national hosts and reflects the reality of broadband networking between and within states. Thus the deployment strategy reflects the desire to encourage broadband networking wherever technically and commercially feasible, with the aim over the medium term to ensure that each island is interoperable in preparation for interconnection over time.

These islands are geographically confined digital broadband nodes offering experimental services to users. Their interconnection allows for the development

Table 6.2 Timetable for deploying TEN-IBC

Phase	Actions during phase
1992–3	Early introduction of business and professional applications; experiments to test new services; procurement decisions on IBC network; completion of standards
1994	Complete interconnection of capitals and neighbouring states
1995	Initial IBC network focusing on business applications
1996	Initial offering of commercial broadband services
1997	Extend IBC to business users in largest conurbations (over 500,000 inhabitants), start of implementing fibre to the home
2005–2010	50 per cent penetration of IBC services

Source: European Parliament

and market testing of transnational services. This strategy reflects the piecemeal development and deployment of TEN-IBC and how concerns of establishing broadband tend to take precedent over wider access and regional development objectives. Initial, albeit limited, trials for the interconnection of networks appear to have been successful.[16] These platforms have enabled equipment manufacturers and users to test relevant aspects of the network. However, demonstration has only been on a limited scale and their use as a model for the full development of TEN-IBC is limited over the short term.

The strategy outlined has direct parallels to previous programmes by seeking to verify, as a precursor to deployment, the standards, technology, regulations and services associated with IBC. This reflects the market realities of the technology, notably with regard to financing requirements, uncertainties over demand and the fast evolving telecommunications market. Any public assistance is designed to minimise commercial risks to operators by manipulating supply conditions and exploiting the mutual interest between broadband islands with regard to the technology. The end point of such actions is to verify the technical and commercial feasibility of the deployment of broadband networks.

The aforementioned strategy is borne of the EU's research initiatives. The development of TEN-IBC as envisaged within the research programmes is reflected in Figure 6.2, illustrating the continuity and consistency between deployment and development of the technology and its practical application and usage under the successive research initiatives.

In addition to these essentially supply-based initiatives, the EU has started to develop specific deployment strategies as a distinct set of separate measures. Specific schemes to aid network deployment are born of the concerns of market forces in this area and of their implications for the technological development of Europe. A key aspect in deployment strategies, especially those aimed at the demand side, is to foster the degree of critical mass required to sustain commercial development. This objective also requires supplementary supply side measures (in addition to research initiatives) to overcome barriers to the marketability of IBC, most notably with regard to its affordability. Consequently much of the reregulation of the sector has to be viewed as integral to the deployment of the network throughout the European socio-economic space.

Specific action upon the deployment of TEN-IBC will eventually be included within the telecom-TENs initiative. The deployment of TEN-IBC within this scheme will be part of a continuation of initial projects to promote TEN-ISDN. It is expected that this initiative will seek to support the spread of the network over the period 1997–9. Much of the deployment work in telecom-TENs will be to stimulate the demand for the IBC network, to establish coalitions, to offer guidance for sources of financial support and generally to develop measures which add rapidity and credence to the process of broadband distribution. The powers under its jurisdiction mean the Commission will be largely a passive actor.

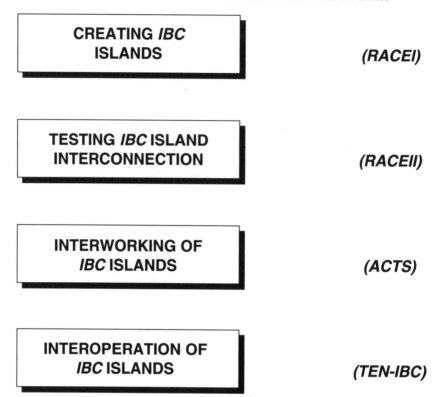

Figure 6.2 Route to deploying TEN-IBC

The ultimate aim is to stimulate investment in the development of IBC in order to aid its realisation on a transnational basis. The priorities of the EU should be to ensure that the lessons of ISDN are be learned and that the assorted networks across the EU, whether national or transnational, should develop in a manner that will enable the goals of interconnection, interoperability and universality to be realised over time.

EMERGING PAN-EUROPEAN BROADBAND NETWORKS

The EU's promotion of IBC as a TEN is complemented by the commercially motivated activities of many PTOs. The desire of PTOs to retain their position within the increasingly liberalised environment has led to assorted, officially sanctioned, collaborative agreements to develop broadband networks in Europe. The synergies between these activities and the objectives of TENs have led to limited support, both implicit and explicit, by the EU. These networks are likely to be pivotal, in one form or another, in the realisation of TEN-IBC. To date there have been a number of collaborative ventures.

Early action to interconnect broadband networks via inter-PTO collaboration took place within the European Broadband Interconnect Trial (EBIT) which was established in 1989. This project, supported by the RACE initiative, was not particularly successful. Wide variations in the tariffs charged, with some offering trial rates and others full commercial rates, combined with a lack of regulatory harmony led to discrepancies in network development. There were also difficulties in establishing harmonised interfaces between states; a symptom of the poor management co-ordination which plagued the trial. By the end of 1992 many of the participants, including the EU, had withdrawn from the scheme, though others did introduce a limited service based upon its results.

The General Electronic Network (GEN) is another joint venture, established in 1990, between the major European operators. It sought to develop a transport network which would eventually offer leased lines of up to 34 Mbp/s between the major commercial centres of Europe. GEN is a direct response by Europe's five largest operators (BT, FT, DT, STET and Telefonica)[17] to the threat of potential entry facilitated by a more liberal regime. The failure of EBIT left a gap in broadband communications to which GEN was, in part, a response. The initial ambitions of the GEN network have been curtailed. The plans for 34 Mbp/s were scaled back to 2 Mbp/s, reflecting initial commercial and technical feasibility.

By the end of the 1990s it is anticipated that GEN will be absorbed into a further PTO collaborative venture: the Managed European Transmission Network (METRAN). The aim of METRAN is to develop a transmission backbone network across Europe based on the technologies of the emerging broadband infrastructure. Most European operators are involved in METRAN as a means of interlinking national networks up to speeds of 155 Mbp/s. The network has faced big managerial problems which were partly derived from the decentralised manner in which it was administered.

The Pilot European ATM Network project (PEAN), a further collaborative venture, aimed to test, in mainly technical terms, broadband services and technology. PEAN is a result of an initial Memorandum of Understanding signed by six PTOs[18] in 1992 to build an ATM network. The pilot, which was partially EU funded, was initially operated for two years and has been utilised to support TEN-IBC projects. PEAN is seen by PTOs as the basis of the European telecommunications backbone network upon which the EII will be based and also as a necessary step for the harmonised introduction of IBC.

By the end of the pilot many felt that it had not achieved the desired breakthrough or significantly influenced carrier implementations, user uptake or the wide-scale commercial availability of ATM. Consequently PEAN is unlikely to form the basis of commercial roll-out of broadband. This has left many commercial users frustrated because there is a general belief that a technological gap is emerging between Europe and its major competitors. Management problems hindered the realisation of any perceptible benefits. Interoperability and interconnection were made difficult by problems associated with melding the equipment from more than a dozen manufacturers. Frequently, the US equipment used operated to different standards from those developed by European vendors. This problem was compounded by a lack of commitment by the major PTOs to the full roll-out of the technology, which may reflect their desire to protect their investments in other less advanced technologies.[19]

Despite this, many PTOs are continuing PEAN under the JAMES initiative, which is partially funded by the ACTS programme. The research network has also combined in a consortium known as TEN-34, which aims to develop networks that operate at 34 Mbp/s. The PTOs feel that the cost of operating such schemes is beyond solely private means and they have turned to the Commission for help.

A further European broadband network is being produced by the Hermes consortium. Its development as a competitor to the incumbent PTOs has been aided by the liberalisation of alternative infrastructure. The plan is to develop a pan-European transport infrastructure based upon fibre optic cabling, utilising the SDH technology (see below), placed alongside Europe's rail network; the rail companies own over two-thirds of the shares in the company.[20] Given that many of the rail partners were already developing their own networks prior to Hermes, it is perhaps no surprise that considerable delay has been experienced. As a result the project only really started to come to fruition six years after it was first proposed. Part of the delay can also be explained by constant movement in members of the consortium.

The establishment of these networks, whether pre-competitive or explicitly commercial, is part of the network of networks comprising TEN-IBC. When interoperable and interconnected, these are the islands that will ensure the seamless flow of telecommunications traffic across borders. Yet it is evident that there is unlikely to be a smooth adjustment to TEN-IBC. The problems experienced by these projects have highlighted the sort of technical and management issues that are likely to be faced by the migration to broadband. Such pan-European projects are complemented by separate national strategies to develop broadband islands which, although conforming to European standards, are being produced in relative isolation across the EU. Any strategy for TEN-IBC has to include them.

NATIONAL INITIATIVES FOR DEVELOPMENT OF BROADBAND NETWORKS

Many states have developed initiatives alongside and complementary to those at European level to push the rapid adoption of broadband networking within their respective economies. Such action reflects the concern that commercial and international activities need to be complemented if the economic benefits of advanced telecommunications are to be felt throughout the economy.

Germany has traditionally led the trials of the technology though its translation into a commercial service has been slow. The trials performed by DT, in line with international standards, aim to develop experience in the field of services, applications, technology and operations at both national and supranational level. This multi-level approach involves developing services and applications at the national level initially, with an international dimension gradually evolving in the most populated areas.

France has perhaps shown the greatest explicit commitment to the delivery of broadband technology to the end user. It was the first state to announce plans for the widespread roll-out of the network. Field trials have been underway since 1993 and FT has sought to promote roll-out via preferential tariffs. FT has collaborated with DT in its network but vast differences in tariff structures still need to be overcome. FT is trying to entice leased line customers to broadband while DT is encouraging take-up generally. The trial has taken place within the forum of the Atlas (now Global One) alliance, which highlights how the PTOs plan to market the network once it is more fully developed.

The strategy of FT has been complemented by the Thery Report (*Network Week*, 1994a) which outlines the French government's position on the national development of broadband infrastructure. This is based upon the delivery of an unlimited number of services. Such a strategy has been heavily criticised by French business and cable companies that look to a more liberal regime to dictate technological development and overcome any relative deficiencies in broadband roll-out. The Thery Report recognises this issue but stresses the importance of public service concerns in broadband network development which could be undermined by rapid liberalisation.

The plan is to establish a fibre optic network that covers every French household by 2015. The estimated cost is FFr150 billion to FFr200 billion for the infrastructure alone. It predicts that FT will meet most of the cost, something about which the company has expressed concern. There is little said within the report about competition although it is difficult to imagine that commercial pressure will not be felt somewhere within the process of network renewal. There is also a general ignorance of the role of other players and of how these plans fit into the evolving pan-European network. It is evident that companies other than the dominant incumbent wish to become involved in network development. This is something which the EU supports, yet there is little evidence that there will be imminent opportunities for them to do so on anything but a limited basis.

The 'Plan Cable', an experiment by the French in ATM network development, launched in 1992, looks a worrying precedent. FFr30 billion was invested and massive losses resulted, which are still evident. Given the poor relative position of French cable roll-out, the government is perhaps placing too much responsibility in the hands of FT. As the technology is still evolving FT sees it as premature to have such a large-scale commitment to investment. Despite the downgrading of indicative planning in France there still seems to be a great attachment to the dirigiste framework in some aspects of the French technocracy.

FT has announced that it is to spend some FFr1 billion upon trial services and projects up to the end of the century. About half the money is to be spent on developing the French fibre optic network to enable it to reach 50,000 to 100,000 houses by the mid–late 1990s. Where possible many of the trials would involve partnerships with French industry, notably alternative infrastructure owners. Thus the government, in spite of the implications of the Thery Report, has started to dilute the idea of FT being solely responsible for broadband deployment and development. Indeed by late 1995 the French government had put forward a bill to facilitate the development of these networks by making conditions more favourable for their success. This bill will allow those involved in trials to deviate from the current legal framework, though for a limited time this will be over a specified geographic space.

In the UK, broadband development and trials reflect a liberal regulatory regime. BT is committed to ATM as the technology of broadband and has undertaken trials in the academic community with the aim of gradually pushing roll-out into commercial markets. To this end it has announced a ten-year programme of work to install fibre optic into homes nationwide. Cable and Wireless has started a broadband service whose primary function is international interconnection for business customers.

Domestically network development is dispersed through a wide range of operators, though the development of broadband services remains largely at an experimental stage. The focus for many operators is on producing commercially viable residential and/or SME broadband services. To this end PTOs and computer groups have set up trials to test interactive services. Sections of the BT trial differ as it is using copper cable to deliver the services. If this works it could revolutionise the understanding of what is actually needed for the information superhighway since it could be developed without the substantial costs of infrastructure renewal. However, initial results highlight that this might be a false dawn as there is only so much which the existing infrastructure can do.

Initiatives by the UK government also reflect its generally non-interventionist stance. As already indicated, the Information Society Initiative[21] has an aim of delivering multi-media services to SMEs within the context of TENs. The British government's view[22] is unashamedly liberal. Like the EU its role is co-ordinative. Therefore trials and applications are more firmly set within the context of market forces than within many other states. The UK's perspective is that these national trials are most likely to be successfully delivered by the private sector within a stable and predictable regulatory framework. The UK government is seeking to influence the roll-out via the deployment of broadband networks to support its own actions. It is hoped that this will act as a catalyst for further technology deployment and development throughout a broader range of sectors.

Over time a consensus between national initiatives is emerging on the means of achieving broadband networks which is broadly similar to that proposed at supranational level. The trials performed have the objective of delivering to national firms, within the context of the development of the EII, advanced services to business. The marketability of these networks is pivotal to their further development and initial deployment. This marketability is likely to deliver the interconnection and interoperability that is central to the realisation of TEN-IBC and the prioritised socio-cultural applications.

National action is not designed to be isolationary but is set within broader supranational and global networks. No state proposes incompatibility. Differences may occur in terms of strategy but the ultimate objective remains the same. In any case there is a gradual approximation of policy at the national level alongside that at the supranational level. Overall these schemes, whether commercial or state sponsored, represent the evolution of the network of networks that is TEN-IBC.

COMMERCIAL DEPLOYMENT OF IBC

Despite the EU's deployment strategy, over the short term the spread of IBC is more likely to occur as a consequence of commercial forces than of any direct policy initiative. The environment within which broadband technology emerges is likely to be pivotal in its deployment throughout networks. The public and private partnerships, which are frequently at the heart of IBC deployment, are asymmetric insofar as much of the investment is likely to stem from commercial sources.

Such asymmetries may hinder deployment due to the nature and degree of risk that commercial operators are expected to bear. An initial estimate of the funding required is some ECU333 billion, which is just for the provision of fibre optic technology to all homes and businesses.[23] Such a figure is inevitably an underestimate for it only includes one aspect of the investment required for the development of the IBC network.[24] The risks associated with deployment are likely to increase as competition becomes more intense; they reflect the embryonic nature of broadband networking. While the demand for broadband within the business sector is relatively certain this represents only a small proportion of the total market. The majority of users (some 75 per cent) are located within the residential[25] sector where demand is extremely unpredictable.

The commercial deployment of broadband technology is inevitably risky. Aside from the deployment of the technology which is agreed by PTOs as the basis of TEN-IBC (i.e. ATM and SDH), many are seeking to deliver services without the mass deployment of broadband technology. Inevitably this is going to involve utilising existing infrastructure.

Deploying broadband via existing infrastructure

Technology is progressing to such an extent that the large-scale renewal of infrastructure may not be needed if existing trials are successful. The ability to use the available infrastructure to supply broadband services could overcome a significant barrier to development and deployment and aid the widespread commercial roll-out and rapid adoption of services to support the information society. In short, compression technologies[26] such as Asymmetrical Digital Subscriber Loop (ADSL) have the potential to alter markedly the economics of broadband networking.

Currently ADSL has been trialled at speeds of up to 8 Mbp/s. Other experiments have extended copper cabling capacity up to 50 Mbp/s, which ties in more closely with assorted broadband technologies such as ATM. A key problem is the lack of broadband access to within the last mile or even less of the home/ enterprise. Compression technologies could feasibly overcome this problem. These copper-based solutions may prove to be temporary, but may be useful market testers to indicate whether large-scale infrastructure renewal via the introduction of fibre into the local loop is commercially viable.

The copper network represents a substantial sunk cost to many operators. Any commercially and technically feasible method of improving its performance and therefore prolonging its life is likely to be welcomed by many PTOs. Despite PTOs trialling the technology many have grown cool on its commercial use due to the realisation that it will be more expensive and problematic than was first thought. Problems posed by the technical nature of digital signals and the lack of a common standard for ADSL have made equipment interconnection and interoperability difficult. Other PTOs have found that ADSL has potentially limited functionality and use cable TV networks to reach a wider market.

Despite these difficulties many PTOs are planning to test ADSL alongside their cable trials, but many are offering greater long-term commitment to fibre optics as a network technology. As such ADSL may only be a transitional technology for the deployment of broadband services. This is certainly a view taken by BT. Due to regulatory restrictions, it does not see that investment in widescale fibre optic network is currently worthwhile, though it will support the ADSL trial. Its position is to offer video-on-demand over copper commercially until regulations are changed and it is able to compete on the same services as cable operators. Recently BT has shown evidence of going cool upon ADSL technology, partly due to the fact that video-on-demand does not appear to be the killer application desired. This is thought to be one of the main reasons why in practice the trial and the technology have been slow to develop into concrete commercial applications. To date only Telia of Sweden has offered compression technologies on a widespread commercial basis.

Deploying the building blocks of IBC: SDH and ATM

The broadband building blocks in Europe will be Synchronous Digital Hierarchy (SDH) transmission and Asynchronous Transfer Mode (ATM) switching. ATM trials have been the focus of many industrial policy initiatives within the EU. SDH, which increases network capacity ten–fifteenfold, is a direct complement to the ATM technology. Commercial SDH investments have been increasing across Europe for some time, aided by a consensus upon its usefulness for evolving broadband networks. SDH has evolved in a series of islands across the EU and as a result is only offering limited capabilities and not fulfilling its potential. As a consequence the delivery of tangible streams of revenue from the technology has been delayed. The deployment of SDH is likely to lead to the opportunities of large-scale restructuring which raise the politically difficult issue of workforce related disorder; as this happens so the infrastructure to support the information society/economy may be hindered.

ATM is much less developed in terms of deployment. ATM will be the transport mechanism of the future and increases significantly the bandwidth available, initially up to 155 Mbp/s but eventually up to an anticipated 622 Mbp/s.[27] ATM is also important as for the first time all aspects of the industry are backing the same protocol and will produce a common platform for all services, future and present, reducing operational cost and enabling new services to be rapidly and universally deployed. Such industry backing is based upon a certainty that ATM will deliver benefits in terms of productivity enhancements, cost reductions and new business opportunities.

Commercial deployment of ATM has been very slow, despite a rapid maturity in the technology. Such reluctance may reflect its potential to undermine the traditional sources of revenue of PTOs and reduce their role in the telecommunications value chain. Additionally the commitment by some PTOs to competing technologies may have persuaded them to delay ATM deployment until revenues are secure. This issue is compounded by uncertainties over tariffs, the technology itself, and the desired speed of roll-out. While ATM has made progress within backbones its relevance for the end user is still doubtful. The technology is used for speedier versions of existing services and not for applications of higher bandwidth that were perceived to justify its enhanced roll-out.

The development of ATM is likely to create a major shift in power within the telecommunications sector. It offers users a single technology for all services and greater choice over equipment and operators. This concern is especially pertinent since it will emerge out of private networks. Thus there is a shift in revenue away from the PTOs towards equipment manufacturers. The end point of such changes is that PTOs could become mere common carriers. Combined with the rise of bandwidth upon demand and other impacts of liberalisation, this has the power to undermine the currently strong commercial positions of PTOs.

European ATM deployment lags behind that of the USA, though research by the ATM forum[28] suggests that the differences between US and EU markets are minimal. Overall the EU is lagging behind the USA by 6 to 18 months in terms of network deployment. Many of the differences are believed to derive from contrasts in regulatory regimes. These can be expected to diminish as Europe liberalises and new competitors for cross-border traffic appear. A major economic difference, which has implications for the outcomes of industrial strategy, is the inflated cost of bandwidth in the EU. This is a pivotal factor in retarding the demand for broadband services but evidence suggests that liberalisation will reduce such disparities.[29] However, the EU may find itself in a paradoxical situation where the liberalisation of markets may simultaneously encourage (via competition) and discourage (via less certain revenues) ATM deployment.

Many operators are deploying ATM, initially at least, as a business solution with seemingly little effort to spread it into broader user groups. It is expected that equipment prices need to fall further to induce an enhanced momentum in deployment into this domain of the telecommunications market. Such economies of scale are unlikely to be available until the demand for the bandwidth offered by ATM has become more mature. This may have to wait until the demand for multi-media renders existing technologies superfluous. ATM has found a home most easily within that segment of the market that has a greater degree of technological sophistication. The education of mainstream users is vital to deployment yet many operators spend time preaching to the converted.[30] The commercial roll out of ATM has been further limited as users have had difficulty in understanding its relative costs and benefits.

The ATM forum, a pre-competitive alliance between interested parties, is seeking to provide impetus to deployment through an active stance on issues such as scheduling and prioritisation of activities. This industry partnership is pushing deployment by focusing upon commercial applications. Its interlinkages with EU plans are unspecified, but instinct indicates that each has separate motives. The actions of the ATM forum are about enabling the technology to attain the desired level of critical mass by focusing upon commercially relevant and feasible applications of the technology. The EU plans to identify critical mass attainment over the longer term in the broader socio-cultural application of the technology.

An installed base of users needs to be expanded before many ATM applications can reach the critical mass required. This is an issue for the technology that has been accepted by industry and policy-makers. It is a pivotal influence upon the EU and the assorted industry forums that are hoping, through their focus on different yet overlapping aspects of the user community, to justify commercial investment in this broadband technology.

While commercial forces are pushing the deployment of broadband technology there is no commitment by operators to develop these networks as true TENs. It is evident that commercial factors are retarding the attainment of critical mass for this sector. EU actions, whether via deployment or research, will assist the process but network operators will ultimately be responsible for IBC. The development of TEN-IBC will need to exploit the investments of the PTOs to achieve its realisation. Consequently critical mass is in the mutual interest of industry and the policy bodies. This still appears to be some way off; so therefore is TEN-IBC. A consequence of such commercial-led deployment is that universality in terms of IBC is a longer term objective. This is further reflected in strategy for the development of the network in the peripheral areas of the EU.

REGIONAL DIMENSION OF TEN-IBC

Despite being a key focus of the EU's industrial strategy, the issue of regional development is not paramount in the establishment of TEN-IBC. The policies initiated reflect the desire to establish the network in Europe as a priority without any specific spatial demands. Thus there is an implicit recognition that IBC will develop at different speeds throughout the EU, a fact recognised as inevitable by the European Commission.

The commercial investment required dictates that networks will develop fastest where there is the greatest density of technologically sophisticated users. The immediate theme of not prioritising peripheral areas for TEN-IBC development does not downplay its perceived importance. Policy-makers realise that to direct operators into cohesion may deter investment in Europe's broadband infrastructure. Despite this initial policy stance, cohesion concerns will remain a longer term objective of policy. The economics of such a decision explain the desire to make TEN-ISDN a platform for the delivery of advanced services in peripheral areas over the foreseeable future – a theme reflected throughout the RACE initiative, despite its objective of the 'harmonious introduction of IBC'. Given the scale of investment required, 'harmony' is unrealistic. This situation recognises that all priorities reflected in the Treaty upon European Union will not be treated equally within IBC network development.

Alternative delivery methods may partially overcome fears of new technological gaps emerging between EU states. Satellite and radio technologies are being utilised to provide cost-effective network access in remote rural areas and in underdeveloped urban areas.[31] To support further access to rural areas, many cable television companies are fostering the development of new technologies such as multi-microwave video distribution systems. The advancement and deployment of these technologies reflect the terrain of the more remote areas of the EU. In addition the BIRD[32] initiative seeks to utilise intermediate technologies such as ADSL to overcome the anticipated deficiency of fibre optic lines for service delivery in peripheral areas. The intention is that such developments will enable the network to support the prioritised telematic applications.

While funding will be available under the telecom-TENs initiative for network deployment, the major supranational R&D schemes are largely unconcerned with cohesion. Many PTOs within the peripheral areas may be collaborating on international trials for broadband communications, but their plans for deployment of the technology are limited compared to advanced states. Given current investment plans for broadband technology and the state of regulation in these states, such a gap is likely to persist.[33]

The Revolve programme[34] highlighted that schemes to promote the regional development of IBC which were not carefully thought out would tend to offer as many benefits to the core regions as they would to peripheral areas. First, investment in IBC in peripheral areas would mean procuring equipment from enterprises in the core, thereby strengthening the relative position of these states and inhibiting the technological development of the periphery. Second, enterprises within the core have a greater familiarity with this technology. This is likely to strengthen their position relative to their peripheral competitors. Such divergences are sustained by political factors such as a reticence to liberalise and more inherent problems such as low user density.

The peripheral states have opted for the slow road to network liberalisation, believing that excessive competition upon relatively immature networks could undermine network integrity and lead to a deterioration of service. Although there are no direct schemes to aid network development, assorted initiatives such as those for SMEs (a common size of enterprise for peripheral regions) and the pilot network projects will, by their nature, assist regional growth. However, it is expected that in these cases network development will still lag behind the more advanced regions of the EU. Evidently an economic culture that is readily able to accept such technology is needed before the sustained roll-out occurs within these regions.

GLOBAL CONTEXT OF TEN-IBC

The development of TEN-IBC is integral to the realisation of a Global Information Infrastructure (GII) via its contribution to the ETSI-defined European Information Infrastructure (EII). Consequently the strategy to develop IBC in Europe partially reflects the desirability of a globally interconnected and interoperable broadband information infrastructure. This is driven in no small part by the desire of many of the PTO-based alliances to develop advanced networks to support the global communication requirements of large users. Such developments highlight the increased interaction and degree of mutual interest between the EU, Japan and the USA in the development of IBC networks.[35]

This mutual interest between the advanced states in the development of broadband is reflected in the G7 pilot projects. Action within these projects is designed to ensure interconnection and interoperability between the different prototype broadband networks being developed by PTOs within the G7 states. The project to ensure the interoperability of broadband is being led by the UK in association with Canada, Germany and Japan. This collaboration is designed to ensure that the results of trials within all G7 states are disseminated. Much of the emphasis to establish collaborative forums is based upon the desire to ensure that the services and applications to support the information society are applicable across borders. The aim is that all future networks should learn from past inconsistencies and be broadly defined on a global level. Such a strategy underlines the increasingly interdependent nature of industrial policy.

The main role of the G7 initiative is not to develop the network but to seek to establish the forums whereby co-operation and collaboration can be effective in realising broadband. As such the work of G7 is to support and complement existing national and international action. The development of the network will include the major carriers,[36] many of whom are slowly rolling the advanced technologies associated with broadband into their networks. Global carriers are seeking to accelerate, with added impetus from the G7 initiative, the roll-out of broadband networks. Their involvement may also enable the trailing of the prioritised applications.

The G7 states are in broad agreement over the framework to achieve the desired level of infrastructure investment. While they recognise the importance of dynamic competition, private investment, a flexible regulatory framework and open access to networks, there are differences in the method of achieving the necessary pre-conditions. The USA is very pro-market, the EU is promoting public/private partnerships and Japan is keen for a greater degree of state direction. Such differences reflect discrepancies in the broadly agreed liberal framework and the relative maturity of telecommunication markets within and between each of the participants.

The Japanese openly dissent from the view that the liberalisation of technology represents the best way forward for these markets, seeing intervention as necessary to attain critical mass. Generally the culture accepts the desirability of state support in pushing the market and in establishing, to a degree of relative maturity, these pre-conditions of Japanese competitiveness. However, MITI has continually expressed fears of the loss of Japan's relative position in the information sector to the USA.[37] In many key indicators Japan is lagging behind the USA, including the number of personal computers and Internet access.[38] Japan is being pushed to follow the strategy of others and liberalise its markets.

Unsurprisingly the USA is taking a much more market-orientated approach to the development of the National Information Infrastructure (NII), its portion of the GII. The USA is the country where the telecommunications market has established the greatest degree of maturity and a culture of sectoral markets has been most firmly established. Where the state does intervene is in terms of a policy steer and in developing applications of socio-cultural importance. Like other initiatives, throughout the globe, it amounts to very little direct action and focuses upon establishing the pre-competitive forums for development of the infrastructure. Many operators are suspicious of any direct involvement by the state, feeling that such action may lead to the state defining the end product as well as working to crowd out commercial investment.

The market-led approach followed by the USA has provided a role model for Europe and highlighted what it does and does not want to achieve via its information infrastructures. A feature of the US model has been a higher rate of penetration of broadband technology into the residential market. This is not an immediate concern of the EU. Recent evidence for the EU is more heartening as in the liberal US market the roll-out of networks is being driven by business not entertainment applications.[39] This contravenes traditional thinking on the way the network would evolve. Many of the large US carriers have stated that the primary purpose of investment in infrastructure was to make business more competitive rather than providing entertainment and online services. The survey indicated that there was little if any support for government funded programmes to develop applications.

The global aspect of the development of TENs is inevitably interlinked to the development of these accompanying strategies. TENs, as a component and complementary policy initiative to the EII and GII, is not and was never intended to be isolated. The experiences of the USA and Japan offer advice for a European strategy. Where there has been heavy state involvement, notably Japan, technological development has tended to lag. A more liberal based approach, such as that followed by the USA, suggests that there is greater scope for advancement. The EU's fear that freer markets without some form of direction would lead to the development of applications that satisfy entertainment requirements and not those of business has not really been borne out by the experiences of the USA. Many groups use the USA as a role model. However, the EU has criticised Japanese and US initiatives[40] for being too narrow and failing to focus upon what it defines as the necessary socio-cultural aspects of the network.

Despite persistent liberalisation there are inherent fractures within the EU's telecommunications environment which potentially limit its ability to offer its enterprises the same advantages as those in the USA and Japan. Many consider that such fragmentation can only be overcome when the liberalisation process has worked its way through. Such inbuilt disadvantages include a diverse heterogeneous market (eight language groups compared to one in the USA), the lack of a single regulatory authority to manage network development, an unevenly spread network and a divergent liberalisation process.

BARRIERS TO DEVELOPMENT OF TEN-IBC

While agreement may exist upon the desired outcome of network development, it is by no means certain that the harmonious conditions to ensure its development as a TEN are in place. It has already been noted above that the Commission recognises as inevitable that the network will develop in a varied manner across space, possibly undermining cohesion concerns and causing further divergences within Europe's socio-economic strata.

In terms of national and international schemes for the co-ordination of IBC networks, the scope for incompatibilities to emerge still persists. While ATM standards are developing they are still sufficiently flexible for incompatibilities to continue. The move towards a multi-vendor environment sharpens the need for a clear set of specified standards. Consequently the development of bodies such as the ATM forum is a positive step. The pace of technological growth and the evolving competitive environment will inevitably demand a standard setting environment that is flexible and complementary to such changes. In such an environment the development of competitive advantage stems from service differentiation, thus excessive standardisation could be detrimental to operators. Consequently standards focus on specific protocols between entities which allow the operators sufficient flexibility to innovate. The failure of markets to develop standards should not be replaced by other failures in terms of technological lock-in due to excessive harmonisation.

While industrial bodies are working to attain such standards, the EU is also acting via the application of ONP to broadband networks to achieve the desired level of interoperability. As yet the application of these rules to broadband remains largely undefined, partly due to the fact that the procedure for ONP to lead to standards remains rather opaque.

Further barriers to the realisation of broadband on a European level are the continued differences in regulations between states, the most notable being regulatory structures that inhibit convergence between relevant sectors. Such convergence is essential if the potential revenues for broadband investment are to be forthcoming. One issue is constraints over what services can be supplied and by whom. Another is the regulation of the sector to prevent an excessive concentration of power by preventing mergers between different players. Part of the problem according to Garnham and Mulgan (1991) is the lack of a common stance on the migration towards broadband; a feature reflected within the regulatory structures of many states. In most states policies to promote network convergence are lacking. Policy has focused upon creating a clear division between different aspects of broadband provision. In part this reflects a desire on behalf of many states to ensure the development of the network in a pluralistic manner. Over time such national differences may disappear as integration proceeds and interdependence between networks becomes more apparent.

As the telecommunications and broadcasting sectors merge, so the regulatory regimes of these sectors may come into conflict. Such difficulties are likely to vary on a state-by-state basis as the degree of separation between cable television and PTOs varies markedly across the EU. Generally both PTOs and cable television companies are keen to protect their key sources of revenue. As the sectors merge the regulators may face resistance from each sector.

Further problems are related to tariff policy. High tariffs are likely to retard network development, while pricing a network that supports a wide variety of services of varying bandwidth is also likely to prove difficult. Pricing the network on a 'per bit' basis may prove to be prohibitively expensive for certain applications such as video on demand. Any reductions in tariffs derived from economies of scale on the mass leasing of lines could lead to cream-skimming and arbitrage. This fear has often meant that PTOs have only offered private circuits reluctantly and where possible have limited the supply. Whether such a strategy would work as Europe moves towards facilities-based competition is doubtful (Stehmann 1995). The issue of tariffs is also complicated where use of the integrated network implies the simultaneous use of services of varying bandwidth. The existing R&D schemes have not really provided an answer to this issue of tariffs. However, it is likely that the decision over tariffs has to reflect the evolving principles of ONP as more operators enter the market.

CONCLUSION

The development of IBC as a TEN, as reflected in the Treaty upon European Union, is not an explicit objective of policy-makers. The initial aim is to establish the development of IBC technology and thereafter plot a strategy for its deployment throughout Europe's socio-economic sphere. Europe's strategy evolves with the technology and the associated standards. This underlines the pragmatic approach that Europe is taking to IBC development. There is no grand vision; it is born of a practical response to changing user requirements.

The success of broadband networking within the EU will be dependent upon the degree of commitment offered to the technology by the PTOs. This implies that the development of a universal broadband network is some way off. The network of networks that is the basis of TEN-IBC is emerging via markets as well as national and supranational sponsored initiatives. At this stage of network development most carriers have now deployed broadband technologies throughout their backbones. Many operators are offering broadband services to large businesses. Their infusion to SMEs remains distant.

Across Europe a number of broadband networks are emerging, many developed by PTO-based alliances and other commercial operators to deliver uniform transnational services to large business users. The focus of these networks makes it difficult to tell how they will fit into the development of TEN-IBC. They are only part of the development of the information society and are based upon offering advanced services to the sector with the greatest technological sophistication. Their application to TEN-IBC, as a support for the broader development of the information society, will really only occur when it is commercially prudent to do so. This raises the issue that the private finance being attracted into the sector is not promoting the development of networks in the desired manner. Consequently the scope for policy measures by national and supra-national bodies emerges to overcome these perceived market failures.

Initial actions in the development of TEN-IBC are focused upon attaining interoperability as a precursor of the widespread interconnection of the assorted islands of broadband across the EU. Universality is currently a lay factor, though once the network is more fully evolved applications developed under the telematics initiative would run over it. Access concerns are centred more upon the delivery of commercial broadband services to the residential market. To this end many PTOs and other operators are developing trials to explore the feasibility of such applications. If these projects prove commercially feasible, new gaps may emerge in technological development between the EU core and periphery.

Overall the strategy chosen by the EU really precludes, over the short term at least, the development of IBC as a TEN. In practice this is the only realistic strategy that can be chosen, given the financial restraints upon public sector activity. The potential contribution that IBC can make to Europe's economic position is substantial, but the ability for it to be realised relies upon a commitment by states to regulate the sector in a manner that enables the funding required to be forthcoming. To date such action has been slow to develop, limiting the potential short-term success of the EU's chosen strategy.

7

CHALLENGES FOR THE EVOLUTION OF TRANS-EUROPEAN TELECOMMUNICATION NETWORKS: CONCLUSIONS

INTRODUCTION

The development of telecom-TENs is integral to the establishment of the information society. Their realisation is based upon a perception of what needs to be undertaken within the European economy to promote the desired economic regeneration and technological transformation. These changes represent a formalisation of trends that has been underway within the European economy for nearly three decades. Policy has pushed the development of ICTs, but only over more recent times has there been a greater focus upon ensuring that they complement the development of the network economy.

Much of national and supranational action towards promoting European competitiveness is based on a series of supply-side measures of which the information society is integral. Policy pertains to seeking the rapid adoption of technology without offering a clear perspective upon the meaning of how rapid this should be and who exactly it should be adopted by.

The liberalisation of trade on a European and global level has exposed the inadequacies of existing infrastructure arrangements. The increased economic interactions fostered by freer trade have increased the interdependence between networks which has highlighted the push for their integration. This integration is born of the desire of enterprises to have uniform functionality across space, requiring networks that are interconnected, interoperable and foster broad access to assorted socio-economic groupings.

The development of TENs focuses upon two migration issues: first, the move to a commonly defined narrowband network represented by the development of TEN-ISDN; second, the migration over time of users to broadband networking. These items are at the heart of the policy challenges posed by the development of the telecom-TENs. An evolutionary approach is generally taken; thus no mass migration of users towards advanced networking is likely to be pursued. This fact is largely determined by commercial considerations. In practice the migration of more users to either form of network is likely to represent some form of technological development. Initially for smaller/lighter users such as the residential, SME and peripheral markets, ISDN is the preferred solution, offering more advanced network functionality which over time may promote a wider shift to broadband networks. The focus on broadband is related to more technologically advanced users such as MNEs. Speculatively, the end point is reached when all users are accessing broadband networks: that is those networks that deliver services at speeds of 2Mbp/s and above.

A MARKET-LED REVOLUTION

The essence of strategy is to encourage commercial operators, via the reregulation of the sector, to deliver the finance necessary to realise telecom-TENs as defined by the Treaty upon European Union. It is already evident that the levels of finance required are not coming forward in the quantity desired. The market's ability to fund the infrastructure undoubtedly exists, the problem being that there seems to be little commercial incentive for this funding to come forward. While the funding gaps are not as significant as in other sectors, they do exist within telecom-TENs and are inhibiting growth in the desired manner. These gaps have already been evident in the development of the EU's immediate priorities for the TENs programme, namely telematic networks and TEN-ISDN. This would seem to indicate that a widespread shift to IBC is distant. The reasons for such resistance on behalf of investors are manifold. Factors such as the sheer scale of investment required, regulatory handicaps (notably with regard to voice telephony) and lack of commercial feasibility of key priority projects have all hindered the flow of investment into the sector.

To date, the technologies associated with the development of telecom-TENs have lacked a critical mass to sustain their commercial roll-out. In part this is due to the fact that technology has advanced beyond the requirements of users and Europe has not fully developed an information culture. This has limited the marketability of the technology and retarded the roll-out of advanced tele-communication networks. The policies of the EU and its states seek to address market failures within the development of the information society. In this context, the market-led approach is complemented by a set of commercially driven policies which stimulate the demand for advanced services. They focus upon market creation and seek to counteract the excesses of the commercial development of networks which could limit successful holistic network development. Initially actions will focus upon attaining the critical mass for TEN-ISDN and TEN-IBC. Such measures are essential if TENs are to be a success but it is too soon to judge results of policy strategy.

Not surprisingly there are disputes over the strategy chosen. Incumbent operators see that protection from market pressures and thus of revenues is the best means of realising the scale of investment required to develop networks as desired. While the inevitability of competition is generally accepted, most seek to limit its extent. Increasingly the perception is that the responsibility of investment needs to be devolved if the required levels of funding are to be forthcoming.

The Commission has been criticised for its presumptive attitude towards the development of TENs. While seeking to free and stimulate the market for these networks, it is trying to determine, in part, what is delivered over it. The focus of the Commission on delivering socio-cultural applications highlights what it believes to be the crucial aspects of market failure and the implications for the realisation of the information society. The policy objective of the control of information has been to ensure that information have and have-nots do not emerge and that users are not exposed to information overload.

The European vision of the information society focuses upon public sector support for socio-cultural applications to overcome the latter form of market failure. By pinning its allegiance to the liberal camp, the EU has potentially undermined its ability to achieve this objective. Clearly commercial actors that are pushed by the profit motive will deliver those applications and services for which effective demand exists. To date such commerciality has tended to be confined to advanced services offered to business users. Other sectors such as residential and SMEs remain underdeveloped. The marketability of ICTs has not been helped by their perceived distance from the end user. New initiatives have sought to address this, yet it is still uncertain how small enterprises and residential users will perceive the relevance of the development of advanced networks.

The gradual restructuring of the sector provoked by market forces is occurring. Most states have lowered monopolistic control of the network and many PTOs are being sold off or restructured as commercial pressure grows. The EU market for telecommunication services is still unevenly developed. The EU is exerting pressure upon states that have failed to implement legislation, or those with derogation to future or ongoing legislation, to remove such inconsistencies. However, the cohesion states remain keen to protect network integrity by delaying the onset of full competition. This raises the spectre of a technological multi-speed Europe. However, even with liberalisation the idiosyncrasies of these markets are likely to have resulted in the emergence of such gaps.

There is very little direct action by the EU in network development. Private–public sector partnerships have been promoted for many aspects of network growth related to telecom-TENs. These imply minimal EU support for the physical infrastructure; focus is upon applications and services. These partnerships seek to attract commercial investment into telecom-TENs via some degree of risk sharing agreement with the public sector. The desire is to offer support to an extent that such projects become commercially as well as technologically feasible. As highlighted above, it appears that public sector support is insufficient to attract the required levels of commercial funding for the priority projects.

The commitment to the technology engendered within the telecom-TENs project has been inconsistent. The Memorandum of Understanding upon

E-ISDN has highlighted one of the evident gaps between the commitment of operators and the desires of policy-makers. These commitments have only been taken seriously when commercial pressures have been exerted on the parties which undertook such a commitment. Common standards still exist alongside national variants of the technology. However, under user pressure many are actively pushing the migration towards common standards. This may bode well for successor networks, notably TEN-IBC.

REALISING THE TENS CRITERIA

The focus of telecom-TENs is on altering the development of public networks. These can offer private services, but if the development of the information society is to occur then these networks need to be accessible to the public as a whole. The belief that the TENs criteria of universality, interoperability and interconnection can be provided holistically by the market is misplaced. Market focus is upon meeting demand for networks with its supply. These TENs criteria are only subsidiary in that they reflect the commercial interests of operators. While interconnection and interoperability may be provided under a liberal regime, universality is likely to be neglected.

INTERCONNECTION

The development of interconnection between different networks is central to the attainment of the network of networks that is TENs. The EU has developed rules of interconnection to enable mobile, satellite and terrestrial networks to be interconnected. Issues of interconnection are largely taken by the PTO and over time, given the development of common standards, this process has been vastly aided. The nationally defined network islands that were part of the development of ISDN in Europe are gradually being removed.

The issue for broadband networks is somewhat disparate. The emphasis lay upon the formation of common standards that reflect the diverse nature of network development of broadband technology. Most states are developing such technology. The challenge is to ensure that they can be interlinked to form an embryonic broadband network. An overall strategy for interconnection does exist. The pressing issue is to establish rules for interconnection within the pluralistic network environment that is emerging in Europe. The development of these rules should open up the market for investment in infrastructure. However, the regulation proposed[1] by the Commission has met with hostility from network operators.

INTEROPERABILITY

The linked issue of interoperability has proved more troublesome. The immediate issue of compatibility of ISDN has to some extent been solved with the development and common acceptance of ETSI standards. Full interoperability will over the short term be limited due to continuation of national standards alongside the common standards. With the renewed enthusiasm among PTOs for ISDN, these differences and incompatibilities should not be overstated. ETSI has been a pivotal factor in aiding interoperability, though it still denies its attainment in some cases due to the sheer time and complexity involved in the standardisation process. The action for the development of standards is based justifiably on the belief that markets would fail to deliver the desired degree of standardisation (OECD 1992).

The issue for broadband networks is more problematic due to the way in which they are developing. Despite pre-competitive agreements between operators these standards need to be more fully fleshed out and can still limit full interoperability. The desire to standardise these advanced networks has to be balanced with the desire to maintain some degree of diversity between enterprises that want both to co-operate and compete. The incentive to do the former may diminish as the latter becomes more apparent. EU policy has sought to promote interoperability by sanctioning as compatible with its competition law a number of competitive and pre-competitive agreements and by using its funding to promote this objective. Even without EU assistance it does appear that network operators have sufficient mutual incentive to collaborate upon these issues as the development of bodies such as EURESCOM and the ATM forum bear witness.

UNIVERSALITY

Much of the focus of policy is upon delivering a set of public services over the advanced communication networks. The aim is that these networks should touch and influence all social, economic and public spheres as a means of promoting sustained network development. The issue of universality is the most evident example of market failure. This provides the essence of the financing problem as the EU is asking the private sector to develop networks that are simply not profitable. Delivering networks to peripheral areas and advancing socio-cultural applications are currently beyond the commercial aspirations of network operators.

In terms of cohesion, past schemes have made a difference to the development of networks but have not perceptibly closed the gap between the peripheral and core regions. Projects such as STAR focused upon the digitalisation and development of ISDN in these areas. Part of the notion of developing ISDN in these regions is a recognition that broadband networks are inevitably going to develop unevenly between core and peripheral regions. The Commission believes that it is better that it should develop somewhere rather than be held back by the public sector seeking to direct investment. Despite this policy stance, the Commission is active in developing applications relevant to rural areas such as teleworking and SME-related services.

144

In terms of the socio-cultural dimension, which is pivotal to the EU's strategy for telecom-TENs, large financing gaps are emerging. In part this is due to the pushing of public service applications in an era when state finances are under pressure. If the main customer for such services is in no position to buy, there seems precious little incentive for the private sector to commit itself to developing applications and services of this nature. These applications, highlighted as central to the EU's conception of the information society, also underline that technology may be running ahead of the practical needs and requirements of users. This may lead to a reappraisal of strategy. The development of mass residential and entertainment services may have to be given priority to enable operators to attain the critical mass required of them to justify this sustained roll-out. From this basis more socially and culturally relevant services could be commercially delivered.

While total universality is not on the agenda, it can be used as a proxy for the desire to spread the utilisation of advanced networks as far as possible to economically relevant users as a precursor to an improvement in economic performance. A feature of the limited universality pursued is to push access to advanced services by SMEs and the labour market. Important as these may be for future economic performance, there is as yet scant evidence from the trials at both national and supranational level that such developments are proving of relevance to the end user.

In the current state of technology the notion of universality, in terms of service, is well understood. How the concept will evolve and be funded is still not fully comprehended as the technology and capabilities of the network mature. The issue of universal service is near the top of the policy-makers' agenda which is not surprising given the importance attached to the information society.

Despite all the talk of the potential of telecom-TENs there still seems to be a great deal of uncertainty surrounding what the evolving advanced telecommunication networks will offer in terms of employment and social scenarios. While policy-makers and technologists expand the hype of the 'information superhighway', its relevance to many is still not fully understood. Clarity of vision is fine but the lack of translation into concrete developments affecting a broad range of economic groups will diminish its desired effects. Part of the problem is that the success of the initiative relies upon actors other than governments to espouse its virtues. If the networks fail to be required by all economic groupings then the networks will not be provided. This is an inevitable peril of the market-based route. Investment will only come forward when the potential of the network is understood and the possible interactions across them are deemed commercially worthwhile to stimulate the required investment. If poor understanding remains, so will market failures.

EMERGING PAN-EUROPEAN NETWORKS AND TENS

There is a clear difference between telecom-TENs as a policy measure and their development as a commercial phenomenon. To date the most evident form of Europe-wide telecommunication networks that is emerging within the EU is associated with the assorted commercial actions of network operators. Thus far these actions have not lived up to expectations. The development of competitive networks has been hindered by regulatory hurdles and consequently has not met the broad aims of the information society. These networks have emerged, initially at least, to satisfy the requirements of a fairly narrowly based community comprised of multinational users. It is as yet unspecified how these will fit into the broader objectives of the information society. Thus, where Europe-wide networks are developing, they are emerging to serve business needs.

Many of these network operators claim that they have already developed TENs. They offer uniform functionality over interoperable and interconnected networks across a broad expanse represented by the European economy. They attribute this development to the liberalisation of the sector that has allowed them to develop pan-European networks as part of their global service. However, these alliances are not as yet direct contributors to the objectives of the information society. This is due to their focus upon closed user groups, the affluent core regions of Europe and the commercial neglect of the prioritised socio-cultural applications.

These business networks are based upon delivering advanced services to large commercial concerns. Their relevance to other user communities is currently not fully understood and is consequently minimal. In part, this reflects the market considerations pushing network development. These competitive networks have been complemented by actions at the pre-competitive level. The rationale for such action is ultimately to define the terms and standards for the development of competitive networks. Thus far progress appears to have been mixed, with some trials not living up to expectations. The perceived importance of these technologies both to policy-makers and commercial operators means that network development will continue. Research policy that brings the technology closer to the user will inevitably help the process.

These pre-competitive arrangements are slowly rolling out the technology, but this is shaped more by commercial concerns. The investment required to roll out these technologies in an environment of increased competition means efficiencies are sought, often meaning labour lay-offs. The political ramifications for enterprises and technological development have yet to be felt. If such restructuring meets with resistance, investments could soon be sacrificed.

The commercial European networks underline how markets are shaping the development of telecom-TENs. This offers a different form of network than that envisaged within the Treaty upon European Union. While it may pursue the TENs criteria, it only does so insofar as these actions are commercially justified. In some senses this highlights the conflict between competition and co-operation in network development.

All the agreements, both competitive and pre-competitive, make the development of networks look very complex and perhaps contradictory. The increased competitive interlinkages between PTOs will further complicate the pre-competitive agreements. The application of technology is a key area where alliances can actively compete. Thus over time collaboration in technological development may become less feasible and ultimately be limited.

POLICY CHALLENGES

Plotting a desired migration path towards advanced networks has to be a key policy objective. Such action will provide greater certainty to commercial operators and users in terms of network deployment and the retraining of labour to cope with anticipated changes. The speed of migration is a derivative of the mutually supporting actions of the public and private sector. While the private sector leads investment, it may look to the public sector to support certain aspects of development to overcome any inertia in the process. Although promoting standardisation, its resources in offering a direct stimulant to the demand for ICTs are limited. In any case such action may be self-defeating if it only manages to strengthen the positioning of Europe's competitors. Therefore action needs to focus upon indigenous network supply and demand. New industrial structures and labour skills may be desired but a clearer policy focus is required. Many European states are developing broadly similar approaches by first creating a greater awareness of ICTs and then, via Europe-wide collaborative ventures, strengthening the positioning of Europe's enterprises in meeting this demand. The action by focusing upon smaller users is seeking to stimulate the critical mass in the market which enables the state to abrogate its role.

Despite pursuing a commercial route to the development of these networks a number of considerations need to be borne in mind in developing telecom-TENs. There should not be an excessive reliance upon market forces. Social solidarity should remain unchallenged; the pain of restructuring today cannot be neglected or excused by the perceived benefits of tomorrow. Public support should be carefully and selectively targeted. According to Stahlmann (1995) policy has thus far failed to address the issues of what the economic, social and political impact of advanced communications will be. Without this basic understanding, the development of the information economy may have to be treated with caution. The experience of ISDN should lead everyone to be more sceptical about much vaunted technology.

Policy therefore remains focused upon provoking change and network development, which means delivering a set of measures that stimulates the supply of networks from commercial sources. This may include support at the individual and firm level to stimulate technological development, supplying better information upon the role and benefits of advanced services and applications and increasing the efficiency, via regulatory changes, of service delivery. Such supply though is only likely to be forthcoming when greater demand has become more evident throughout Europe's socio-economic strata. These concerns are broadly addressed within the network management role that the public sector, at regional, national, supranational and international level, is establishing for itself in the process of network development and deployment.

The process for the establishment of TENs is well developed. The rules for development are written centrally but enforced on a local basis. As a result issues related to the TENs criteria are still set locally; there is no obligation to meet them. These criteria are a desired outcome and there is nothing obligatory in their attainment. Where they have been pushed is because of commercial pressure. The broad framework that is initiated by the EU is established in detail by states which leaves open the possibility of discrepancies.

While TENs reflect the growing interdependence between national telecommunication networks there are further challenges as the process of globalisation continues. This means the desire for uniform functionality on a global level and collaboration with global rivals upon networks of mutual interest. These factors are likely to be strengthened once the World Trade Organisation agrees to free up the trade in telecommunication services. Already the mutual interest of states and other operators in global networks has been reflected in the G7 initiatives and the formation of global alliances. The information society is likely to be global, as will the networks to support it. The success of such developments is still dependent upon the support given to them by operators.

CONCLUSION

Over time it is expected that the physical network will decline in importance as the focus shifts to the content of what it delivers. The actions of software and broadcasting companies are clearly concentrated upon delivering added value to enterprises. Policy-makers equate improvements in information infrastructure with advancements in international competitiveness. These are beliefs that are almost uniformly shared and explain the expanding number of schemes at national and international level. The challenge is to translate these benefits from theory into practice. A particular problem arises when the technology appears to be ahead of the needs and requirements of users. Thus far the longer term ambitions of telecom-TENs have been overtaken by the short-term realities of the market, a natural result of many operators seeing TENs as part of a global business not a public service.

NOTES

1 TRANS-EUROPEAN TELECOMMUNICATION NETWORKS AND THE RISE OF THE INFORMATION ECONOMY

1 There have been many initiatives by states and the EU in this area. For fuller details see Chapter 6 on TEN-IBC.

2 This is the definition given by the OECD, as quoted in the Commission of the European Communities, 'An Industrial Competitiveness Policy for the European Union'.

3 As quoted in *Agence Europe*, 09/11/94.

4 As quoted in Sharp (1993) 'Industrial Policy and Globalisation', in Hughes, K. *Future of UK Competitiveness and the Role of Industrial Policy*, Policy Studies Institute.

5 See Cowling in Hall G. (1986) p.206.

6 'European Industrial Policy for the 1990s', *Bulletin of the European Communities*, Supplement, 3/91 and 'An Industrial Competitiveness Strategy for Europe', *Tech Europe*, Supplement, October 1994.

7 Ibid., p.12.

8 Commission of the European Communities (1993b).

9 See Johnson and Turner (1997) Chapter 1.

10 See European Round Table of Industrialists (1990) p.2.

11 See Bressand and Nicolaidis (1990) pp.27–49.

12 Commission of the European Communities (1996).

13 The impact of these factors upon the competitive process is explored more fully in Chapter 2.

14 See Chapter 1.

15 As noted in Greenop (1995).

16 There are conflicting perspectives upon this, given the desire for a market-led route to network development. The basic premise is that ICTs should be seen to be working for the betterment of society and not its titillation.

17 See Capello and Nijkamp (1991).

18 A fuller analysis of these events can be explored in Drucker (1993).

19 See Knieps (1987).

20 See Capello (1994).

21 Generally this would include information providers, service providers, network operators, as well as hardware and software manufacturers.

22 For an analysis of the role of telecommunications infrastructure in economic development, see Saunder (1994).

23 See Commission of the European Communities (1993b).
24 See Keen and Cummins (1994).
25 As featured in Antonelli (1992).
26 Ibid.
27 For the purposes of this book narrowband is defined as transmission speeds of 2 Mbp/s and below. Anything above this is considered to be broadband.
28 See Commission of the European Communities (1995b).
29 For a full list of applications that are deemed to be of common interest see Commission of the European Communities (1995b) p.31.
30 Ibid. Article 129b paragraph 2.
31 Common carrier implies non-discrimination between network users for whom it makes facilities available upon demand to other service vendors and users. Such neutrality must extend through to content as well as types of user and operator.

2 TELECOMMUNICATIONS, INDUSTRIAL COMPETITIVENESS AND THE EMERGING NETWORK ECONOMY

1 A notable case is in the development of telecommunications in Europe where intra-firm networks are sanctioned by the EU (see later).
2 As noted in Nijkamp et al. (1994) Chapter 1.
3 Increasingly networks are being seen as an intermediate form of economic organisation between markets and hierarchies. For further analysis see Thompson et al. (1987).
4 As quoted in Steinfeld et al. (1994) p.204.
5 For figures see Commission of the European Communities (1994g) (part II).
6 See Chapter 3.
7 See Jacquemin and Marchipont (1993) p.21.
8 Ibid., p.20.
9 Commission of the European Communities (1994a) p.21.
10 Ibid., p.21.
11 See Capello (1994) p.102.
12 Ibid.
13 There are parallels between this process and Myrdall's model of regional development.
14 Papers presented at the OECD Workshop on the Economics of the Information Society, University of Toronto, 28–29 June 1995 (OECD 1995b).
15 Morganti F./Databank Consulting, Remarks prepared for the OECD Workshop on the Economics of the Information Society.
16 This growth rate is incremental and therefore must be added to already anticipated trends in output growth.
17 'Economic Benefits of the Administration's Legislative Proposals for Telecommunications', report to White House 1994. As quoted in OECD (1995b).
18 Both of these reports are cited in OECD (1995b) pp. 52–53.
19 See the assorted evidence presented to the House of Lords European Communities Select Committee (1994).
20 As quoted in Capello (1994).
21 This point of view is closely associated with the work of Robert Solow.
22 This is a claim espoused by Paul Krugman.
23 See OECD (1995b).

3 THE STRATEGY AND INDUSTRIAL FRAMEWORK FOR TRANS-EUROPEAN TELECOMMUNICATION NETWORKS

1 Bangemann M. (1996) 'The European Vision of the Information Society', 10th World Congress 'Technology and Services in the Information Society', 3 June 1996.
2 This collaboration is not sector specific. It can occur between private sector actors, public sector actors and as part of a partnership between the two sectors.
3 A common feature of the initial stages of cable deployment by companies in the EU has been the large losses they have incurred. In part such losses are derived from regulatory restrictions.
4 See Public Network Europe (1994b) p.38.
5 A fuller analysis of ISDN is in later chapters.
6 See Council Recommendation Concerning the Implementation of Harmonisation in the Field of Telecommunications 84/549/EEC.
7 European Strategic Programme for Research into Information Technologies.
8 *Green Paper on the Development of a Common Market for Telecommunications Services and Equipment* (1987).
9 According to Stehmann (1995) the difference is that in the former (service-based competition) services are provided over a common network. In the latter a supplier's services are provided over its own facilities.
10 Such evidence could be derived from the losses made by cable operators in the EU who were unable to offer voice telephony.
11 This has certainly proved a key retardant on the roll-out of cable television networks.
12 Generally the availability of high capacity leased lines is greater in the more liberal markets. This is true for other indicators of telecommunications infrastructure development such as number of digital lines and access to cable TV. For full details see *Communications Indicators for Major Economies 1995* (1996) Eurostat.
13 This has generally been the experience of the USA.
14 Wik Report on Interconnection and Arthur Andersen Consultancy.
15 This is the collective name for Spain, Portugal, Greece and Ireland.
16 See *Public Network Europe* (1996a) p. 40.
17 The major alliances are Atlas, Uniworld, Concert and Cable and Wireless.
18 Notably Cable and Wireless envisages the beginnings of roll-out by 2010.
19 Of note here is the collaboration between France Telecom with Cap Gemini and Sema which underlines the convergence between telecommunications and computing.
20 European Virtual Private Network Association is a group of largely US multinational companies that sought to use their leverage to obtain discounts upon telecommunication services provided by the competitive alliances.
21 See, for example, the case of the regulatory restrictions placed upon the Global One alliance.
22 SITA was originally a network designed to meet the needs of airlines.
23 An alliance between France and Deutsche Telecom to provide value added services.
24 BT's outsourcing arm.
25 Unisource relied upon SITA to deliver global functionality.
26 ATM is Asynchronous Transfer Mode; this is a broadband transmission technology.
27 Frame Relay is an improved means of data communications.
28 VPNs are Virtual Private Networks. These are voice-centric technologies associated with intelligent networking.
29 The MoUs will be dealt with in more detail in later chapters.
30 The European Institute for Research and Strategic Studies in Telecommunications.

31 Committee for European Post and Telecommunications.
32 For an analysis of this see Reddy (1990).
33 International Telecommunications Union.
34 See 'Court of Auditors Attacks Programme Directors', *Tech Europe*, March 1994, Section II, pp.3–4.
35 European Committee for Standardisation.
36 European Committee for Electrotechnical Standardisation.
37 European Community Telecommunications Users Association.
38 European Telecommunications Network Operators.
39 Many of these are core states, notably Denmark and the Netherlands.
40 Denmark and others have speeded up the process of liberalisation to release commercial funding; others such as Spain look like following. Only Greece is proving reluctant and is receiving aid to upgrade its network to remove fears of competition.
41 This can be seen in the manner with which the EU has used competition laws to deal with a number of competitive alliances, notably the Atlas deal between Deutsche Telecom and France Telecom.
42 See CEC (1991a) *Guidelines on the Application of EEC Competition Rules in the Telecommunications Sector* (OJ C 233, 6.9.91).
43 The local loop is the connection from the user's premises to the main network.
44 See Hudson (1994).
45 Special Telecommunications Action for Regional Development.
46 This has been complemented by the actions of other bodies such as the European Investment Bank.
47 Such assistance can come via the Structural Funds, the Cohesion Fund or via the TENs Budgetary Line.
48 A clear case in point is the UK, where there are evident disparities between the south-east of England and the rest of the UK.
49 For a full analysis see *Report of the Sixth Strategic Review Committee on European Information Infrastructure*, ETSI 1995.
50 This is the figure quoted in the *White Paper upon Growth, Competitiveness and Employment* and already appears to be a gross underestimate.

4 THE INTEGRATED SERVICES DIGITAL NETWORK AS A TRANS-EUROPEAN NETWORK (TEN-ISDN)

1 This fact is true for basic rate access. The more advanced primary link requires a fibre optic link.
2 Data compression is a technology that seeks to fit broadband services within narrowband capacity.
3 See, for example, evidence submitted to the House of Lords European Communities Select Committee (1987) by Matson and other members of the cable industry.
4 Basic rate access has limited functionality and is targeted at SMEs and the residential market. The primary access has greater bandwidth and is designed to support corporate applications of up to 2 Mbp/s.
5 Prior to the adoption of the new Euro-wide standard, BT's network was based upon the DASS 2 signalling system.
6 M. Carpentier (1990) 'The European Commission's Policy for ISDN development', *Computer Networks and ISDN Systems*, Vol. 18, No. 2, p.150.
7 D. Shorrock (1990) *Telecoms Users Guide to Networks*, Comm End Publishing.
8 The term is derived from European Communications Newsfile (1993a).
9 Such services include Internet access and Frame relay.

10 This is offered by many PTOs under the banner of bandwidth upon demand.

11 European Communications Newsfile (1993a), p.14.

12 BT was forced to modify its tariff reductions for ISDN on the complaints of competitors.

13 Though BT's ISDN-2 developed initially as an international service its functionality to users was limited due to the incremental nature of interlinkages.

14 See (86/659/EEC).

15 See (89/C 196/04).

16 See European Round Table of Industrialists (1990).

17 Eighteen PTOs signed the MoU: PTT Austria, Belgacom, TeleDanmark, TeleFinland, ATC Finland, FT, DT, OTE (Greece), Telecom Eireann, Tele-Italia, P&T Luxemburg, PTT Telecom Netherlands, Telecom Portugal, Telefonica (Spain), Telia (Sweden), Swiss PTT Telecom, BT and Mercury. By the end of 1995, 26 PTOs had signed the MoU.

18 ISDN MoU Implementation Management Group.

19 The development of these new services has been given the backing of a number of large equipment manufacturers, notably Alcatel, AT&T, GPT and Ericsson.

20 The actual patterns of migration and introduction to E-ISDN are noted elsewhere in this chapter.

21 Modems are a means of transforming analogue signals into digital form.

22 Norme Européenne de Telecommunications (NETs).

23 Common Technical Regulations.

24 This is in effect a practical expression of the principle of mutual recognition that lay at the heart of the SEM.

25 See Progress Report of the Approximation of the Laws of Member States concerning Telecommunications Terminal Equipment COM(96)114.

26 APIs are software for accessing and administering ISDN services. The importance of APIs has arisen due to the increase in PCs as a means of communication over the network.

27 Trans-European Network ISDN.

28 The aim is to close the economically important telematic gap (see later).

29 The TEN-Telecom initiative was established to provide an holistic and integrated framework for the establishment of generic services and applications to be delivered by TEN-ISDN. These will eventually aid the migration to TEN-IBC (see later).

30 Initially the EU was given ECU7 million for both broadband and narrowband schemes. The total cost of their development will run into billions of ECUs. The *White Paper upon Growth, Competitiveness and Employment* (CEC 1993b) puts the figure at ECU15 billion over the five years up to 1999. This figure is likely to be an underestimate.

31 *European Report*, No.1937, 26 March 1994. This figure includes SMEs but excludes the residential market which is likely to enhance the figure.

32 Such forums include the Committee TEN-ISDN and the European ISDN Users Forum.

33 The call proposals highlight these two broad areas as the core concern. Citizen networks includes socio-cultural applications; SME networks are based upon delivering generic services to this form of enterprise.

34 See *European Report*, No.1937 26 March 1994, p.11.

35 Communication from the Commission upon the Development of ISDN as a Trans-European Network COM (93) 347.

36 Sectors include education and training, healthcare, transportation and rural development.

37 See CEC (1992). DG XIII, p.4.

38 See contribution by Ewbank Preece to European Conference of Telematics Proceedings, 1993 (CEC 1993g).
39 For a full analysis and experiences see STAR and Télématique conference reports which indicate in more detail the regional impact of these schemes.
40 See evidence presented at the Télématique Conference Proceedings (CEC 1991b).
41 See CEC (1993g).
42 The regions involved are the Free State of Sachsen (Germany), the Community of Valencia (Spain), Nord-Pas de Calais (France), Central Macedonia (Greece), Piemonte (Italy) and the North West of England.
43 The Inter-Regional Information Society Initiative.
44 Better Infrastructure for Regional Development.
45 The Event 'Global '95', which sought to demonstrate the application of ISDN in a globally harmonious manner, chose ETSI standards as the means of delivery.
46 Over the period 1993 to 1996, basic rate access monthly rental has fallen markedly. The price for primary access has barely changed over this period. These figures were based upon a comparison of ten states.
47 Philips started offering a VPN service to SMEs, traditionally only affordable to large companies in 1994.
48 Information in such a format could be provided by, for example, mail order firms or banks.
49 See evidence submitted by Matson to the House of Lords European Community Select Committee (1987).
50 See Commission document on infrastructure liberalisation (Part II) (CEC 1994g).

5 TRANS-EUROPEAN TELEMATIC NETWORKS

1 For an analysis of these and other issues involved in the application of telematics to transport see Soekka (1990).
2 The development of TENs draws a distinction between these two. Economic viability refers to the 'general long-term socio-economic profitability of a project'. This is broader than financial profitability which is the commercial reward obtainable from a project.
3 See Commission of the European Communities (1993) *Trans-European Data Communications Networks between Administrations* COM(93)69.
4 Co-operation in Automation of Data and Documentation for Imports/Exports and Agriculture.
5 Inter-Institutional Integrated Services Information System.
6 Trade Electronic Data Interchange System.
7 See Ridge (1994:131).
8 For details see *European Report*, No. 1992, 11 November 1992, Section IV, p.5.
9 The programme for Trans-European Services for Telematics between Administrations.
10 The initiative STEPS (Solutions for Telematics in Public Services) openly promotes an open forum for consultation in network development.
11 These conclusions were drawn from Commission of the European Communities (1994c).
12 See Commission of the European Communities (1993d). The SME services prioritised are file transfer, E-mail, generalised access to databases, videophone and group 4 fax.
13 Regional Infrastructure for Teleworking in Europe. This scheme is part of the telematics programme and ran from 1994 to 1995.

14 This is evident from the details given in the European Telematics Conference in 1993 (CEC 1993g). Papers presented from different areas highlighted these positive impacts; this generally applied to many regions.

15 Inter-Regional Information Society Initiative.

16 The selected applications are those highlighted previously as in the common interest.

17 Process Engineering Trends for Public and Private Organisations Requiring Integrated Telematics Applications.

6 TRANS-EUROPEAN INTEGRATED BROADBAND TELECOMMUNICATION NETWORKS (TEN-IBC)

1 See Commission of the European Communities (1995b).

2 This definition, although simplistic, is quite commonly used by the EU.

3 Such a vision of the network is offered by Greenop *et al.* (1994).

4 A local area network is one that operates within a narrowly defined territory such as a building or between a group of users usually no greater than 5 km apart. A wide area network is one that operates beyond this limited geographical area.

5 See Denmead and Ablett (1994) p.73.

6 This backbone was developed under the Eureka-funded project COSINE. This was a pan-European telecommunications infrastructure for research, industrial and governmental communities.

7 These are broadly reflected within previous chapters.

8 See Adonis (1995), p.34.

9 This was the basis of a point made by Matson (1987) in evidence presented to the House of Lords Select Committee on Telecommunications Policy.

10 *Public Network Europe* (1994b) pp.33–38.

11 Commission of the European Communities (1993e).

12 For example, Visinet and Idea.

13 SONAH aims to develop services to interconnect national hosts.

14 See Kruger (1995) pp.119–121.

15 Commission of European Communities (1996) *ACTS 2000 Plus* (Brussels) is a document developed as a result of a study by DG XIII to examine research issues beyond the current ACTS scheme.

16 See Commission of the European Communities (1995) *Demonstration of Inter-working via Optical Networks*, COM(95)342.

17 The initial scheme was limited to these five, though it has been extended to others.

18 BT, FT, DT, Telefonica, STET, Iritel.

19 See 'European ATM Pilot Comes up Short', *Communications Week International* 28/11/95, p.2.

20 The two participants are GTS (Global Telesystems Group), a US company, and Hit Rail, a consortium of 11 railway companies.

21 The Information Society Initiative is essentially an awareness campaign designed to stimulate the demand for advanced telecommunications within SMEs.

22 This is reflected within the UK government DTI *Command Paper upon Information Superhighways*, Command Paper No. 2734.

23 This was the result of calculations conducted by the consultancy firm KPMG for the European Commission.

24 This estimate does not include the investment perceived as necessary in the development of nodes or services.

25 See Adonis (1995), p.96.

26 This includes technologies such as Asymmetrical Digital Subscriber Line (ADSL) and High Bit Rate Digital Subscriber Loop (HDSL). The technology works upon

compressing high bandwidth applications to the extent that they can pass through narrowband copper networks.

27 Over the longer term it is anticipated that ATM could offer speeds up to 10 Gigabits per second.

28 See ATM Forum (1995).

29 The Dutch and German public network operators are notable examples of carriers that have substantially lowered the cost of broadband leased lines (34 Mbp/s).

30 This was the result of a survey carried out by the consultants Analysys (1995).

31 The Race project CATALYST has shown that broadband can be offered over satellite links.

32 Better Infrastructure for Regional Development.

33 See Ovum Report *ATM in Carrier Networks* (1995).

34 Revolve Report (1988).

35 The Strategic Audit of RACE in 1993 highlighted the desire that such research initiatives should have a global dimension. This includes participation by non-EU companies in the programmes, a greater responsiveness of EU PTOs to global requirements of EU enterprises and increased global co-operation in R&D.

36 For example, BT, AT&T, Sprint.

37 ETSI estimates that the USA has a five- to ten-year advantage in the development of this sector.

38 'Japan's Infrastructure is Falling Behind', report in *Network Week*, 6 June 1995.

39 Mark Rockwell (1996) 'Business Drives National Information Infrastructure, Survey Says', *Communications Week*, 26 February 1996 (Source: Reuters Business Database).

40 See J. Riley, 'Japan and US Allow Chances to Slip through the Net', *Computer Weekly*, 18/05/95, p.18.

7 CHALLENGES FOR THE EVOLUTION OF TRANS-EUROPEAN TELECOMMUNICATION NETWORKS: CONCLUSIONS

1 See Commission of the European Communities (1995) *Proposal for Interconnection in Telecommunications* COM(95)379.

BIBLIOGRAPHY

Adams F. and Klein L. (eds) (1983) *Industrial Policy for Growth and Competitiveness*, Lexington Books.

Adonis A. (1995) *Network Europe and the Information Society*, Federal Trust.

Allen D. (1988) 'New Telecommunications Services', *Telecommunications Policy*, Vol.12 No.3, pp.257–270.

Analysys (1995) 'ATM: The Message That Must Get Through', *Telecoms Strategy Update*, Issue 7, Summer.

Anonymous (1991) 'Memorandum of Understanding for the Implementation of an European ISDN Service by 1992', *Computer Networks and ISDN Systems*, Vol.21, pp.69–74.

—— (1996) 'Tomorrow's Network, Tomorrow', *The Economist*, 20 April, pp.27–78.

—— (1996) 'Commission Moves to Inject Cash into Telecoms Applications First and Attract Investment Later', *European Voice*, 29 February, p.20.

Antonelli C. (ed.) (1992) *The Economics of Information Networks*, North-Holland.

—— (1994) 'Localised Technological Change and the Evolution of Standards as Economic Institutions', *Information Economics and Policy*, Vol.6 Nos. 3–4, pp.195–216.

Arlandis J. (1994) 'ISDN: A European Project', in Steinfield C., Bauer J. and Caby L. (eds) *Telecommunications in Transition*, Sage.

ATM Forum (1995) 'Wide Area Deployment in Europe: White Paper', The ATM Forum European Market Awareness Committee, ATM Forum Webserver.

Bangemann Group (1994) *Europe and the Global Information Society*, Brussels.

Bangemann M. (1992) *Europe's Industrial Policy*, Kogan Page.

Baquiast J-P. (1993) 'Trans-European Administrative Networks', *Annales des Mines*, December, pp.37–38.

Bator F. (1958) 'The Anatomy of Market Failure', *Quarterly Journal of Economics*, pp.351–379.

Baumol W. (1965) *Welfare Economics and the Theory of the State*, Bell.

Baumol W., Panzer J. and Willig R. (1982) *Contestable Markets and the Theory of Market Structure*, Harcourt Brace Jovanovich.

Baumol W. and Willig R. (1987) 'Contestability: Developments since the Book' in Morris D. *et al. Strategic Behaviour and Industrial Competition*, OUP.

Bell D. (1976) *The Coming of the Post-Industrial Society*, Basic Books.

Bianchi P., Cowling K. and Sugden R. (eds) (1994) *Europe's Economic Challenge*, Routledge.

Blankert C. and Knieps G. (1993) 'State and Standards', *Public Choice*, Vol.77 No.1, pp.39–52.

Booty F. (1994) 'ATM Currently a Long Day's Journey into the Night', *Communications Network*, September, pp.29–30.

Borthwick R. and Stehmann O. (1994) 'A Strategy Towards Infrastructure. Competition in the European Union', *Telecommunications Policy*, Vol.18 No. 8, pp. 616–628.

Bressand A. and Nicolaidis K. (eds) (1989) *Strategic Trends in Services: An Inquiry into the Global Services Economy*, Harper and Row.

—— (1990) 'Regional Integration in a Networked World Economy' in Wallace W. *Dynamics of European Integration*, Pinter.

Briscoe P. (1993) 'ATM: What Does it Promise?', *Telecommunications*, September, pp.49–52.

Brunn S. and Leinbach T. (1992) *Space and Time: Geographic Aspects of Communications and Information*, Harper Collins.

Bubley D. (1994) *Opportunities for ISDN*, Financial Times Management Reports.

Burton F. (1995) 'Residential Broadband Services: A European Study', *British Telecommunications Engineering*, Vol.14, pp.250–257.

Cane A. (1995) 'Competition Down the Line', *Financial Times*, 19 January, p.20.

Capello R. and Nijkamp P. (1991) 'Telecommunications as a Catalyst Development Strategy', Paper presented at the Urbinno Workshop on the Future of European Cities: the Role of Science and Technology, Vienna, October–November.

Capello R. (1994) *Spatial Analysis of Telecommunication Network Externalities*, Avebury.

Carmo Seabra M. (1993) 'Telecommunications', *European Economy*, No.1993/no.3, pp.287–312.

Carpenter B. (1991) 'The Importance of Pan-European Broadband Networks', *The Interoperability Report*, pp.9–13.

Carpentier M. (1989) 'The European Commissions Policy for ISDN Development', *Computer Networks and ISDN Systems*, Vol.18, pp.149–154.

Carpentier M. (1993) 'Telecommunications and Telematics Networks in Europe', *Annales Des Mines*, December, pp.6–10.

Cave M., Milner C. and Scanlon M. (1994) *Meeting Universal Service Obligations in a Competitive Telecommunications Sector*, Commission of the European Communities/ DG IV.

Chapman P. (1996) 'ACTS Lays Info Society Highways', *European Voice*, Vol.2 No.7, p.20.

Chesnais F. (1988) 'Technical Cooperation Agreements between Firms', *STI Review*, No.4.

Ciborra C. (1992) 'Alliances as Learning Experiences' in Mytelka L. *Strategic Partnerships and the World Economy*, Pinter.

Clark M. (1991) *Networks and Telecommunications*, John Wiley and Sons.

Clyne L. (1994) 'Report from the ATM Task Force', *Computer Networks and ISDN Systems*, Vol.25, Suppl.3, pp.S135–S139.

Coase R. (1960) 'The Problem with Social Cost', *The Journal of Law and Economics*, Vol.3, October.

Commission of the European Communities (1990a) *Europe's Industrial Policy in the 1990s* COM(90)556.

—— (1990b) *Towards Trans-European Networks* COM(90)585.

—— (1990c) *Directive 90/388/EEC on Competition in the Markets for Telecommunications Services*.

—— (1991a) *Guidelines on the Application of EEC Competition Rules in the Telecommunications Sector* OJ C 233, 6/9/91.

—— (1991b), *Télématique: Conference Proceedings* DGXIII/DGXVI.

Commission of the European Communities/Council of the European Communities (1991) *Treaty on European Union*.

—— (1992) *STAR: Programme Report* DGXIII.

—— (1993a) *Communication to the Council and the European Parliament on the*

Consultation of the Review of the Situation in the Telecommunications Services Sector COM(93)159.

—— (1993b), *White Paper Upon Growth, Competitiveness and Employment* COM(93)700.

—— (1993c) *Re-enforcing the Effectiveness of the Internal Market* COM(93)256.

—— (1993d) *Proposal for a Council Decision Adopting a Multi-annual Community Action Concerning the Development of ISDN as a Trans-European Network (TEN-ISDN)* COM(93)347.

—— (1993e) *Preparatory Actions in the Field of Trans-European Networks: Integrated Broadband Communications* COM(93)372.

—— (1993f) *Trans-European Data Communication Networks between Administrations* COM(93)69.

—— (1993g) *European Conference on Telematics: Conference Proceedings*, Crete, October.

—— (1994a) 'An Industrial Competitiveness Policy for the EU', *Bulletin of the European Communities*, Supplement 3/94.

—— (1994b) *Solutions for Telematics in European Public Services* DGXIII.

—— (1994c) *Telematic Systems of General Interest* COM(94)185.

—— (1994d) *An Action Plan for the Information Society* COM(94)347.

Commission of the European Communities/DG XIII (1994e) 'More Competitive Industry Through Research' *I&T Magazine News Review*, Autumn.

—— (1994f) *Green Paper upon the Liberalisation of Telecommunications Infrastructure and Cable Television Networks (Part I)*, 25/10/94.

—— (1994g) *Green Paper upon the Liberalisation of Telecommunications Infrastructure and Cable Television Networks (Part II)* COM(94)682, 25/01/95.

—— (1994h) *Progress Report 1993 concerning the Co-ordination of the Introduction of ISDN in the European Union* COM(94)81.

Commission of the European Communities/DG XIII (1995a) 'Trans-European Broadband Networks: Eliminating the Roadblocks', *TEN-IBC Conference Proceedings*, 11/07/95.

—— (1995b) *Towards the Information Society* COM(95)224.

—— (1995c) *On the Status and Implementation of Directive 90/388/EEC*, COM(95)113.

—— (1996) *Benchmarking the Competitiveness of European Industry*, DG III, 9/10/96.

Cone E. (1995) 'Global Services', *Communications Week*, 20 March, pp.57–63.

Confland D. (1993) 'Information and Competitiveness', *Annales des Mines*, December, pp.63–65.

Costello J. (1991) 'Testing Requirements for ISDN', *Public Network Europe*, March 1991, pp.53–56.

Coulter M. (1996) 'Brussels Does the Right Thing – Telecoms Technology', *Electronic Times*, 25 January.

Council of the European Communities (1992) 'Resolution on the Development of ISDN in the Community as a European Wide Telecommunications Infrastructure for 1993 and Beyond' 92/C158/01, Brussels.

Cowling K. and Tomam H. (eds) (1990) *Industrial Policy After 1992: An Anglo-German Perspective*, The Anglo-German Foundation.

Cullis J. and Jones P. (1987) *Micro-economics and the Public Sector*, Blackwell.

Curzon-Price V. (1986) *European Industrial Policy*, Macmillan.

David P. and Greenstein S. (1990) 'The Economics of Compatibility Standards', *Economics of Innovation and New Technology*, Vol.1, pp.3–41.

David P. and Steinmuller W. (1994) 'Economics of Compatibility Standards and Competition in Telecommunication Networks', *Information Economics and Policy*, Vol.6 Nos.3–4, pp.217–243.

Delcourt B. (1991) 'EC Decisions and Directives on Information Technology and Telecommunications', *Telecommunications Policy*, February, pp.15–21.

Delmas R. (1993) 'Information and Communication Sciences', *Annales des Mines*, December, pp.66–70.

Denmead M. and Ablett S. (1994) *Network Europe: Telecoms Policy to 2000*, Analysys Publications.

Department of Trade and Industry (1995) *Creating the Superhighway of the Future: Developing Broadband Communications in the Future*, Command Paper No.2734.

Devlin G. and Bleackley M. (1988) 'Strategic Alliances: Guidelines for Success', *Long Range Planning*, Vol.21 No.5, pp.18–23.

Dodgson M. (1993) *Technological Collaboration in Industry*, Routledge.

Dosi G. (1988) 'Sources, Procedures and Micro-economic Effects of Innovation', *Journal of Economic Literature*, Vol.26, pp.1120–1171.

Drucker P. (1993) *Post-Capitalist Society*, Butterworth Heinemann.

Duchane F. and Shepard G. (1987) *Managing Industrial Decline in Europe*, Pinter.

Economides N. (1993) 'A Monopolists Incentive to Invite Competitors to Enter in Telecommunications Services' in Pogorel G. (ed.) *Global Telecommunications Services and Technological Change*, Elsevier.

Economides N. and Himmelberg C. (1994) 'Critical Mass and Network Evolution in Telecommunications', Working paper, Stern School of Business, New York University.

Economides N. (1995) 'The Economics of Networks', Working paper, Stern School of Business, 1995.

Egan B.L. (1991) *The Information Superhighway: The Economics of Advanced Public Communication Networks*, Artech House.

European Communications Newsfile (1992) 'How PTOs are Reacting to the Changes in European Telecoms', Vol.4 No. 4, pp.14–16.

—— (1993a) 'Can Euro-ISDN Kick Start the Market?' Vol.5 No.7, p.14.

—— (1993b) 'France Telecom: Leading the Way in ISDN Provision', Vol.5 No.12, p.10.

European Parliament/Directorate General for Research (1993) *Emerging Technologies: Information Networks and the European Parliament*, Economic Series, W-11.

European Report (1994) '1998: The Year for Liberalising Infrastructure', No.1994, 19 November, Section IV, pp.13–15.

European Report (1995) 'Van Miert Sticks to his Guns', No.2088, pp.11–13.

European Round Table of Industrialists (1990) *Missing Networks: A European Challenge*, ERT Brussels.

Ewbank Preece (1993) *Proceedings from the European Conference on Telematics*, Crete, October.

Farrell J. and Saloner G. (1985) 'Standardisation, Compatibility, and Innovation', *Rand Journal of Economics*, 16, pp.70–83.

—— (1992) 'Convertors, Compatibility, and the Control of Interfaces', *Journal of Industrial Economics*, Vol.40 No.2, pp.9–36.

Federation of the Electronics Industry (1994) *Trans-European Networks*, Discussion paper.

Fiske J. (1994) 'Regulating Telecommunications', Proceedings, Centre for Regulated Industries Conference, *Utilities Law Review*, Summer, pp.83–84.

Foldvary F. (1994) *Public Goods and Private Communities*, Edward Elgar.

Francis A. and Tharakan P. (1989) *The Competitiveness of European Industry*, Routledge.

Franzmeyer F. (1982) *Approaches to Industrial Policy in the EC and its Impact in European Integration*, Gower.

Freeman C. and Perez C. (1988) 'Structural Crises of Adjustment' in G. Dosi, C. Freeman, R. Nelson, G. Silverberg and L. Soete *Technical Change and Economic Theory*, Pinter.

Friedmann W. (1971) *The State and Rule of Law in a Mixed Economy*, Stevens and Sons.

Fuchs G. (1992) 'Integrated Services Digital Network: The Politics of European Telecommunications Network Development', *Journal of European Integration*, Vol.16 No.1, pp.63–88.

Galbraith J. (1958) *The Affluent Society*, Hamish Hamilton.

Gannon P. (1991) 'Pan-European ISDN', *I&T Magazine*, No.2, pp.24–25.

Garnham N. and Mulgan G. (1991) 'Broadband and the Barriers to Convergence in the European Community', *Telecommunications Policy*, Vol.15, pp.182–194.

Garric C. (1994) 'An Enlightening Look at Policy Development', *I&T Magazine*, No.13, pp 6–9.

Gilbert R. (1992) 'Symposium on Compatibility', *Journal of Industrial Economics*, Vol.40 No.1, pp.1–9.

Gillespe A. (1993) *Proceedings from the European Conference on Telematics*, Crete, October.

Gilhooly D. (1991) 'Shaping Telecoms Towards 1992', *Communications Week International*, September–October, pp.34–41.

Greenop D. (1995) 'Shaping the European Information Society', *British Telecommunications Engineering*, Vol.14, October, pp.186–195.

Greenop D., Pearson I. and Johnson T. (1994) 'Broadband-Liberating the Consumer', *British Telecommunications Engineering*, Vol.12, January, pp.252–259.

Hall G. (ed.) (1986) *European Industrial Policy*, Croom Helm.

Hall G. (1986a) 'The Theory and Practice of Innovation Policy: An Overview' in Hall P. (ed.) *Technology, Innovation and Economic Policy*, Phillip Allan, pp.1–34.

Handel R. (1994) 'The Future of ATM in Deregulated Markets', *Telecommunications*, June, pp.59–60.

Hardisty A. and Harris M. (1994) 'Harmonising Leased Lines in Europe', *Telecommunications International*, July, pp.27–34.

Helm D. (ed.) (1992) *The Economic Borders of the State*, OUP.

Hills T. (1994) 'Making SDH Real', *Communications International*, November, pp.76–79.

House of Lords European Communities Select Committee (1994) *Growth, Competitiveness and Employment*, Seventh Report, HMSO.

Huber R. (1991) 'Designing Europe's Broadband Future', *I&T Magazine*, No.2, pp.6–8.

Hudson H. (1994) 'Universal Service in the Information Age', *Telecommunications Policy*, Vol.18 No.8, pp.658–667.

Hughes K. (ed.) (1993) *The Future of UK Competitiveness and the Role of Industrial Policy*, Policy Studies Institute.

I & T Magazine (1994) 'The Information Society: the Way Ahead', Winter 1994–95.

Information Market Observatory (1994) *ISDN in the European Union* DG XIII, IMO Working Paper 94/1.

Jacquemin A. and Marchipont J. (1993) 'New Challenges Facing Community Industrial Policy', *Annales des Mines*, December, pp.20–24.

Jacquemin A. and Sapir A. (1990) *The European Internal Market: Trade and Competition*, OUP.

Janelle D. (1991) 'Global Interdependence and its Consequences' in Brum, S. and Leinbach, T. *Collapsing Space and Time*, Harper Collins, pp. 49–81.

Jarillo J. (1988) 'On Strategic Networks', *Strategic Management Journal*, Vol.9, pp.31–41.

Johanson J. and Mattsson L. (1988) 'Internationalisation in Industrial Systems – A Network Approach' in Hood, N. and Vahine, J.E. *Strategies in Global Competition*, Routledge.

Johnson D. and Turner C. (1997) *Trans-European Networks: The Political Economy of Integrating Europe's Infrastructure*, Macmillan.

Jonscher C. (1983) 'Information Resources and Economic Productivity', *Information Economics and Policy*, Vol.1, pp.13–35.

Jouet J., Flichy P. and Beuad P. (eds) (1991) *European Telematics: The Emerging Economy of Words*, North Holland.

Katz M. and Shapiro C. (1985)· 'Network Externalities, Competition and Compatibility', *American Economic Review*, Vol.75 No.3, pp.424–440.

—— (1986) 'Technology Adoption in the Presence of Network Externalities', *Journal of Political Economy*, Vol.94, pp.822–841.

—— (1992) 'Product Introduction with Network Externalities', *Journal of Industrial Economics*, Vol.40 No.1, pp.55–84.

—— (1994) 'Systems Competition and Network Effects', *Journal of Economic Perspectives*, Vol.8 No.2, pp.93–115.

Keen P. and Cummins J. (1994) *Networks in Action*, Wadsworth.

Knieps G. (1987) 'The De-regulation in Europe: Transportation and Telecommunications' in Majone G. *De-regulation or Re-regulation*, St. Martin's, pp.72–100.

Koebel P. (1987) 'De-regulation of the Telecommunications Sector' in Majone G. *De-regulation or Re-regulation*, St. Martin's, pp.110–123.

Koenig K. (1994) 'ISDN: An Essential Component in Trans-European Networks', *I&T Magazine*, No.11, pp.16–19.

Koustoulas I. (1986) *A Competitive Future for Europe*, Croom Helm.

Koutsoyannis A. (1979) *Modern Micro-economics*, Macmillan.

Kruger P. (1995) 'Is This the Final ACT for the EC before the Internet Wins All?', *Telecommunications International*, September, pp.119–121.

Lambarelli L. (1995) 'Comparison of European and US Market Trends in ATM Implementation' (Parts I and II), ATM Forum, European Market Awareness Committee Working Paper.

Lamberton D. and Neumann K-H., (1994) 'The Economics of Standards', *Information Economics and Policy*, Vol.6 Nos.3–4, pp.193–194.

Landaburu E. (1993) 'Regional Development in Europe', *Annales des Mines*, December, pp.27–29.

Law C.E. (1990) 'ISDN Moves Ahead in Europe Slowly', *Business Communications Review*, Vol.20 No.13, pp.88–92.

Ledyard J. (1976) ' Discussion on the "Nature of Externalities"' in Lin, S. (ed.) *Theory and Measurement of Economic Externalities*, Academic Press.

Littlechild S. (1978) *The Fallacy of the Mixed Economy*, IEA.

Macdonald S. (1992) 'Information Networks and the Exchange of Information' in Antonelli, C. (ed.) *The Economics of Information Networks*, North-Holland.

Mackenzie D. (1994) 'Testing Time for Europe's Broadband Future', *I&T Magazine*, No.13, pp.10–13.

Majo-Cruzante J. (1991) 'EC Policy to Promote High Speed Networking for Research in Europe', *Computer Networks and ISDN Systems*, Vol. 21, pp. 233–238.

Malchup F. (1962) *The Production and Distribution of Knowledge*, Princeton.

Mansell R. (1994) 'Strategic Issues in Telecommunications', *Telecommunications Policy*, Vol.18 No.8, pp.588–600.

—— (1995) *The New Telecommunications*, Sage.

Matson J. (1987) 'Evidence Presented before the House of Lords' in House of Lords European Communities Select Committee (6th Report) *European Telecommunications Policy*, HMSO.

Matutes C. and Regibeau P. (1988) 'Mix and Match: Product Compatibility without Network Externalities', *Rand Journal of Economics*, Vol.19 No.2, pp.219–234.

BIBLIOGRAPHY

Mohan-Reddy N. (1989) 'Industrywide Technical Product Standards', *R&D Management*, Vol.19 No.1, pp.13–25.
Mohan-Reddy N. (1990) 'Product Self-regulation: A Paradox of Technology Policy', *Technological Forecasting and Social Change*, Vol.38, pp.39–63.
Monk P. (1992) 'The Economic Significance of Infrastructural IT Systems', *Journal of Information Technology*, Vol.8, pp.14–21.
Musgrave R. (1958) *The Theory of Public Finance*, McGraw Hill.
Musher A. (1993) *The Migration Path to ATM*, Report by Technology Applications and BIS Strategic Services.
Nelson R. (1987) 'Roles of Government on the Mixed Economy', *Journal of Policy Analysis and Management*, Vol.6 No.4, pp.541–557.
Network Week (1994) 'France Telecom Reveals ATM strategy', 14 November, pp.1–4.
—— (1994a) 'French Government publishes Digital Highway report', 14–18 November, pp. 1–4.
Nicolaidis P. (ed.) (1994) *Industrial Policy in the Community: A Necessary Response*, Kluwer.
Nijkamp P., Vleugal J., Maggi R. and Masser I. (1994) *Missing Transport Networks in Europe*, Avebury.
Noam E. (1990) *Telecommunications in Europe*, OUP.
Norton J. (1990) 'Threats and Opportunities in Pan-European Communications', *Telecommunications*, March.
OECD (1992) *Technology and the Economy*, Paris.
—— (1995a) 'The Global Information Infrastructure', *OECD Observer*, special issue, No.196, October–November.
—— (1995b) *Workshop on the Economics of the Information Society*, Workshop No.1, Toronto, June.
—— (1996) *Workshop on Information Infrastructure and Regional Development*, Proceedings, Paris.
Olsen E. and Rogers D. (1991) 'The Welfare Economics of Equal Access', *Journal of Public Economics*, Vol.45, No.1, pp.91–105.
Olson M. (1965) *The Logic of Collective Action*, Harvard.
Ovum Consultancy (1993) 'ATM in Europe', *Value Added Services in Europe*, pp.162–165.
Ovum Consultancy (1994) *E-ISDN: A Users Guide*, Ovum Publications.
Ovum Outlines (1995) *Broadband Networking*, Ovum Consultancy, No.2.
Patel V. (1992) 'Speeding Toward a Single Market', *Communications International*, January, pp.43–46.
Perrot A. (1993) 'Compatibility, Networks and Competition', *Transportation Science*, Vol.27 No.2, pp.62–72.
Porter M. (1990) *The Competitive Advantage of Nations*, Macmillan.
Price C. (1977) *Welfare Economics in Theory and Practice*, Macmillan.
Public Network Europe (1991a) 'Can ISDN Cross National Borders?' April, pp.43–46.
—— (1991b) 'Early Days for European ISDN', March, pp.48–52.
—— (1993a) 'European ISDN: Launching This Year', March, pp.57–59.
—— (1993b) 'Europeans Seek Evidence from ATM Trials', December 1993–January 1994, pp.31–34.
—— (1993c) 'Trans-border Push for ISDN', September, pp.61–65.
—— (1993d) 'Can ATM Follow SDH into Europe?', June, pp.59–64.
—— (1994a) 'SDH and ATM: Time for Action?', June, pp.59–63.
—— (1994b) 'The True Price of Industrial Policy', April, pp.33–38, Economist Publications.
—— (1995a) 'ATM and SDH: More Problems and Solutions', March, pp.57–61.

—— (1995b) 'ISDN's Future in the Coming Broadband Age', November, pp.61–66.
—— (1995c) 'TENs: Work Horse or Trojan Horse?', September, pp.47–52.
—— (1996a) 'Don't Expect Perfection', March, pp.39–42.
—— (1996b) 'TENs: Vision and Reality', Vol. 6 No.7, pp.41–44.
—— (1996c) 'Is ATM All It's Cracked Up to Be?', March, pp.27–31.
—— (1996d) 'Dirigisme: Thanks, But No Thanks', February, pp.39–42.
—— (1996e) 'ISDN Sees European Growth', September, pp.25–30.
Reddy N. (1990) 'Product Self Regulation', *Technological Forecasting and Social Change*, Vol.38, pp.49–63.
Reddy N., Cort S. and Lambert J. (1989) 'Industry Wide Technological Product Standards', *Research and Development Management*, Vol.19 No.1, pp.13–25.
Revolve Report (1988) 'Constraints and Requirements on the Introduction of Integrated Broadband Communication into Less Favoured Regions of the European Community', *Race Project No.1028*, Second Report 25/11/88.
Ridding J. (1995) '$200 Million Boost to French Superhighway', *Financial Times*, 10 March, p.8.
Ridge M. (1994) 'Towards a European Nervous System', *Public Administration*, Vol.72, Spring, pp.127–134.
Rietbroek J. (1993) 'EC Initiatives upon Trans-European Networks', *Information Economics and Policy*, Vol. 5, pp. 287–294.
Rosenburg N. (1982) *Inside the Black Box: Technology and Economics*, Cambridge University Press.
Rothwell R. (1983) 'The Difficulties of National Innovation Policies' in Macdonald S. *et al.* (eds) *The Trouble with Technology*, Pinter.
Rowley C. (1975) *Welfare Economics*, Martin Robertson.
Roy M. and De Sousa P. (1994) 'Integrated Broadband Communications in Europe', *Telecommunications*, November, pp.29–33.
Saint-Hilaire P. (1995) 'European ATM Pilot Works Towards International Interoperability', *ATM Forum*.
Santucci G. (1994) 'Information Highways Worldwide: Challenges and Strategies', *I&T Magazine*, No.13, pp.14–23.
Saunder D. (1994) *Telecommunications in Economic Development*, World Bank.
Sauter W. (1995) 'Taking the Parallel Tracks of European Telecommunications Regulation into the Future', *Utilities Law Review*, Winter, pp.142–145.
Schenker J. (1995) 'A New Public Network Model', *Communications Week International*, 2 October.
Schumpeter J. (1942) *Capitalism, Socialism and Democracy*, Harper and Row.
Schwartz M. (1987) 'The Nature and Scope of Contestability Theory' in D. Morris, P. Sinclair, M. Slater and J. Vickers *Strategic Behaviour and Industrial Competition*, OUP.
Scitovsky T. (1954) 'Two Concepts of External Economies', *Journal of Political Economy*, Vol.62.
Schenker J. (1992) 'Euro-Broadband Net Set', *Communications Week International*, 20 July, p.3.
Seldon A. (1990) *Capitalism*, Basil Blackwell.
Shand A. (1984) *The Capitalist Alternative*, Wheatsheaf.
Shorrock D. (1989) *European Communications*, Blenheim.
Shull S. and Cohen J. (1986) *Economics and Politics of Industrial Policy*, Westview Press.
Soekka H. (ed.) (1990) *Telematics, Transportation and Spatial Development*, VSP.
Stahlmann M. (1995) 'The Trouble with the NII – The National Information Infrastructure is an Exercise in Irrelevancy', *Information Week*, 26 June.
Stehmann O. (1995) *Network Competition for European Telecommunications*, OUP.

BIBLIOGRAPHY

Stehmann O. and Borthwick R. (1994) 'Infrastructure Competition and the European Union's Telecommunication Policy', *Telecommunications Policy*, Vol.18 No.8, pp.601–615.

Steinfeld C., Bauer J. and Caby L. (eds) (1994) *Telecommunications in Transition*, Sage.

Stoneman P. (1987) *The Economics of Technology Policy*, Oxford.

Streeton H. and Orchard L. (1994) *Public Goods, Public Enterprises and Public Choice*, Macmillan.

Swann D. (1983) *Competition and Industrial Policies in the EC*, Methuen.

Sweeny T. (1994) 'ATM Trial Operators Confront Limitations', *Communications Week International*, 12 December, pp.19.

—— (1995) 'European ATM Pilot Comes Up Short', *Communications Week International*, 28 November, p.3.

—— (1995) 'Copper Loop Breaks 50 Mbp/s Barrier', *Communications Week International*, 1 September.

Systems Synthesis (1995) *Regional Infrastructure for Teleworking*, July.

Teece D. (1995) 'Telecommunications in Transition', *OECD Conference on the Economics of the Information Society*, Toronto, 28–29 June.

Telecom Markets (1995) 'BT Finally Set for Commercial Video-on-demand Trial', No.271, p.1.

—— (1995b) 'Europe's TOs Go Cool on ADSL Despite Lining Up Trials', No.264, pp.13–17.

—— (1995c) 'ATM Set to Take Over the World – But Not Just Yet', November, No.280, pp.10–12.

Thompson G.F. (1990) *The Economic Emergence of a New Europe*, Edward Elgar.

Thompson G., Frances J., Levacic R. and Mitchell J. (1987) *Markets, Hierarchies and Networks*, Sage.

Thorelli H. (1986) 'Networks: Between Markets and Hierarchies', *Strategic Management Journal*, Vol.7, pp.37–51.

Tirler R. (1990) 'The EBIT Project', *Computer Networks and ISDN Systems*, Vol.19, pp.299–303.

Tsoukalis L. (1993) *The New European Economy*, OUP.

Tucker E. (1994) 'Brussels Closes Off a Multimedia Gateway', *Financial Times*, 10 November, p.2.

Valdar A., Newman D., Wood R. and Greenop D. (1992) 'A Vision of the Future Network', *British Telecommunications Engineering*, Vol.11, October, pp.142–151.

Valiant S. and Rosenburg R. (1993) 'Evolving Private Networks in Europe', *Telecommunications*, April.

Van Tulder R. and Junne G. (1988) *European Multi-nationals in Core Technologies*, Wiley.

Williams M. (1982) 'Industrial Policy and the Neutrality of the State', *Journal of Public Economics*, Vol.19 No.1, pp.73–96.

Williamson O. (1989) 'Transaction Cost Economics' in R. Schmalensee and R. Willig (eds) *Handbook of Industrial Organisation*, Vol.1, North Holland.

Wu A., Cattarius D., Roy M. and Vinckier R. (1994) 'RACE, Integrated Broadband Communications and Interworking', *Euro Abstracts*, Vol.32, No.8, pp.518–524.

INDEX